The Jesus I Always Wanted to Know

D. Sundarsingh Moses

The Jesus I Always Wanted to Know
by D. Sundarsingh Moses
Published by *Global Action*
7660 Goddard Street, Suite 200
Colorado Springs, CO 80920, U.S.A.

www.globalaction.com
o: 719.528.8728; f: 719.528.8718

ISBN: 978-1-4507-4704-2

Published in the United States by *Global Action*

Cover design: Barten Visual Communications, www.bartenvisual.com
Interior design: Nasko D. Lazarov

Printed in the United States of America
2010 - First *Global Action* Edition

Content

Part V: Impact Beyond the Church Walls

Introduction

SUNDAR MOSES IS ONE OF THE MOST UNUSUAL PEOPLE I have ever met. In January 2000, I had the privilege to speak for a week in his church in Lucknow. We became good friends. As you will read in this book, I have observed God using him in mighty ways. I have also had the privilege to work alongside him, observing him up close. Sundar Moses is the real thing!

Sundarsingh Moses was born in Tuticorin, in the southern part of Tamil Nadu, India, on November 23, 1961. His father is a retired banker and his mother is a retired schoolteacher. He grew up in a home with two siblings.

After attending school and eventually graduating from university with a Masters degree in Economics, he served the Government Bank for ten years. Sensing God's calling on his life, he studied at Trinity Theological College in Singapore for three years and graduated with a Master of Divinity degree.

As a member of the Methodist Church in India, Sundar was asked to become the pastor of the English-speaking congregation that meets at Lal Bagh Methodist church in Lucknow. This is the church that was pastored by the well-known missionary, E. Stanley Jones, the author of *Christ on the Indian Road* and the founder of the Christian form of ashrams.

In 2007 Sundar Moses was given a leave of absence from the Methodist Church. Since then he has served *Global Action* in various positions such as full-time lecturer for the Global Module Studies (GLOMOS) program as well as the National Director for India. He and his wife, Angeline, have three children; David, Esther and Lydia. They live in Lucknow, Uttar Pradesh, India.

This book is not a biography in the true sense of the word. But through these stories about the life of Sundarsingh Moses, you will sense God's way of working in his life, year after year, in location after location. The world is waiting to run into him, but more importantly run into Sundar's God!

A book like this does not happen by itself. A special thanks to the editor, who spent hours turning this book into English after its "Indian Swenglish" origin, and to Nasko Lazarov who ensured that each page was designed properly.

Lars Dunberg
Colorado Springs
November 2010

Part I
The Beginning

The Crossroad

THE BEST THING THAT HAPPENED IN MY LIFE WAS when God took it and changed it. Even though I was born in a Christian family, nothing significant happened until that change took place in my heart.

For 21 long years we went to church, heard some of the best sermons, saw peoples' lives changed and were part of a church that experienced great exponential growth.

But it was not until October 1983 that God entered my life. I was a student in Madras Christian College in South India. I was living my own life. It was a horrible life. I was completely frustrated because I could not be free. I always thought to myself, "If I can get into something, I can get out of it." That is not true! Friends and habits and everything that make a person bound, enslaved me. While I lived this life I did not know who to talk to or with whom I could share my frustrations. I began to ask basic philosophical questions.

What is the meaning of life? What do I want to do with my life? As a student, what should I do next? Get a job? Then what? Save money? Get married? And then? Have children? Then what? Buy a motorbike? A car? A house? Every time you pay off one loan, you take on a bigger one. Before you know it, you are ready to repeat the process in the next generation. You tell your children to be exactly like you, and then what? Sit in my rocking chair, drink coffee and read the newspaper waiting for my turn? Is this what life is all about? Is there something more? If this is all there is, why live this life at all? Why not terminate it?

And so, I found a philosophical answer. Death is the solution to life! Little did I realize that I was in a process of self-destruction. I asked people why they did what they did. I went to parties and talked to people who were drunk. I talked to young people high on drugs and asked people if they enjoyed anything in a relationship? I was not satisfied. I was pursuing the truth, if there was such a thing as truth. Strangely, I found myself giving a farewell speech to all my friends. I said, "Life is not worth living. I am going to terminate my life!" And, do you know what? Not even one of them said to me, "Don't take this drastic step!"

I expected somebody would make me feel important, to give me a hug or attempt to persuade me to reconsider this decision. Nothing happened. I went home crying. Were these people really my friends? Weren't these the people, the friends, that I was willing to do anything for? If this was not friendship, then what relationships did I have in this world?

Simultaneously and unknown to me, a man of God visited our home. He had come to pray for my aunt who was suffering with a serious illness. While he prayed for her, he suddenly stopped in the middle of the prayer and in a loud voice, said, "Sundar! Sundar! My son, what are you doing?" My parents were present at that prayer time. Their hearts were broken. They began to weep. My dad asked the man, "What are you talking about?" The man responded, "Your son is in real trouble, but don't worry, God will help him. God has a great plan for his life."

My father could not really understand. Somehow I had managed to hide my entire life from him. I tried to be the best son my father could ever have, but I knew I was the worst hypocrite on planet earth. I dreaded seeing him. Such a good man having such a horrible son! I had no answers to the predicament that I was in. How long would I play this game? I hated loneliness, privacy, and the night. I felt so guilty, so broken, and so hopeless.

That night my father stood waiting at the end of our street. Somebody had been sent to ask me to come home. "Your dad wants you to come home. Come quickly!" As I was in the middle of my farewell speech, I took some more time to finish my conversation and then walked home, only to see my father standing there at the end of the street, crying. I never understood Luke 15 until that moment. I knew I was the prodigal son. Did I come home transformed? No, I came home as a rebel. My dad told me, "There is a man here, waiting to pray for you." I hated Christians. I hated prayer. I hated people who talked about God.

The man asked me, "Can I pray for you?" "Go ahead" I responded. I wondered why people prayed. He placed his hands on my head and said; "I see death in your face." I was shocked! I had never seen this man before. How would he know about my life? A few minutes ago I had been talking about a death sentence I was going to inflict on my own life. I had pretended to be an actor all my life, so I put on one more act. Finally, he was gone. I stayed awake thinking about it all through the night.

Two days later I was invited to a prayer meeting. I don't know when I made the decision to go, when I got ready or how I got there. I thank God for the temporary loss of memory on that episode. I thought to myself, *what harm can it do to attend a Christian meeting? I can protect myself.*

With this feeling I went to the meeting. I sat there as they sang songs over and over. They even sang in slow motion as they repeated phrase after phrase. *Is this what Christians do? Why would they do these funny things?* I thought. I did not belong there.

A man stood up to speak. It was the same man who prayed for me at my home! I remember vividly that he spoke from Matthew 8 and Matthew 14. Matthew 8 tells the story of Jesus walking on the water. The boat was full of water and the disciples were crying out, terrified. They were fisherman, and that was their strong point. They cried out for help because they had never experienced a problem so big in their entire life. I could identify with that! The second story, found in Matthew 14, describes Jesus sleeping in the boat. The disciples cried out, "Master, don't you care! We are drowning." I could identify with that too. In my heart I cried to God. Who will help me? I am drowning. I don't even have courage to tell anyone that I am drowning. I don't have the answer.

This man said, "You may have tried everything but maybe you have not tried Jesus." I knew he was talking to me. I didn't know this Jesus. I had heard about him but I did not know him. I said to myself, *Whoever you are, if you are God, if you really are who this man claims you to be, save me! Save me! Change my life. I hate this wretched life. Set me free. I have tried so hard. I will not try one more time. If you are God, I want you to change me.*

I don't know if that was a prayer. I did not raise my hand. I did not go forward at the invitation. I did not know anything about Christian things, but this I knew. I cried from my heart, hoping that whoever this Jesus was, he would hear me. The process broke my heart. I could not imagine that Christian services were so draining. When the speaker began to speak, I felt the words cutting my heart into pieces. I didn't want to be hypnotized, so I took my chair and put it behind a concrete pillar, but the word found me. I cried like never before. I was ashamed of crying publicly, but I knew that something wonderful and powerful was taking control of my life.

That night one of my cousins who was with me at the meeting said, "Why don't we go forward? We can be prayed for." Quickly I responded, "I don't believe in this stuff, this prophecy, people talking about the future, people using the name of God. I don't believe this stuff." My cousin encouraged, "It won't harm you, come. Let's go forward, let's just be prayed for."

As I went forward, brother John Joseph looked at me, and said, "God has chosen you to be his servant. He will take you north, south, east and west across the oceans. You will be a witness for Christ, and you will be a fool for Christ." My eyes were wide open and I was laughing inside. *They have started their old game again, these Christians! These so called prophecies, these so-called hearings from God* I thought to myself. Now I know. I was the fool who could not believe in the God who could do the impossible.

Oh! The peace of God, the peace of God. That night I slept like never before. The next day I woke up to a new day and a new chapter in my life. I felt like a colorful butterfly; light, flying, enjoying the freedom and freshness of life. I realized what it means to have the joy of salvation, to be relieved of my burdens.

At that moment I knew I must share what happened in my life with others. I knew my journey had begun. It all started that night in October 1983, when as a twenty one-year old I stood at the crossroad of life. I thank God for the Cross on that road.

The Influence

FOR THE MOST OF MY LIFE I GREW UP IN AN EXTENDED family. We spent time together, enjoyed playing sports and went on a lot of family outings together.

There was one person who was very instrumental in making sure that we experienced the awesome work of God in our lives. This person was my father's elder sister, Jessie Moses. She was an outstanding Christian. As we observe people in general we may say, "They're good from afar but far from good." Sometimes it might seem that the closer you get to people you tend to see things differently than what you see in them from a distance. But, this was not the case with my Aunt Jessie Moses. She was good from afar, and too good when you came close to her. She was an outstanding person who dedicated her whole life to God. She remained single all her life and worked for the cause of education. More importantly, her heart was focused on influencing people for Christ.

Jessie Moses began her career as a teacher in a school founded by some Scottish missionaries in Chennai. When she took charge of the leadership in the school, it had approximately 65 students. By the time she retired, the institution had grown to more than 3,500 students. More important than the number of students was the quality of their education. Jessie was building lives, instilling the character of God in them and leading so many to Christ through her influential position.

Her influence extended to our family too. She was an outstanding person in her private and professional life. It was Jessie who initiated our family gatherings with a view to introducing each member of the family to Jesus.

Every Sunday we went to church for the morning and evening services. We were more interested in getting together for pleasure than for fellowship at my aunt's home. We sang songs and, of course, my aunt prayed because nobody dared to pray. She prayed relentlessly and persevered in praying for every need and for every person. These were such long, intense prayers that some of us dozed off to sleep. But we woke up quickly at the end of her prayers when she brought goodies from her refrigerator. Being the head of an institution and a well respected person in the city meant that she received loads of "stuff" which she was more than happy to share with us. Often we had potluck dinners. We thoroughly enjoyed our fellowship on Sundays, often ending the day so late that it was well past midnight when we finally returned to our homes.

Now and then Aunt Jessie would bring servants of God, gifted and anointed by the Holy Spirit, to come and share the message. What they taught was not different from the teaching we heard in church, but it was delivered with a passion that was contagious. I somehow felt that the fire and the passion at church were not always contagious. During these prayer meetings, one by one God touched the lives of the older ones and the younger ones in the family. It became so meaningful. It was in these meetings that I first had the opportunity to share my faith in Christ after being born again. What a joy to part of it! It was an amazing thing God accomplished in the lives of my family members, like a revival fire that raged through every family. We all came to know the Lord in many different ways.

A young woman in her late teens hailing from the neighboring state of Andhra Pradesh was used by God mightily. Over the years she had become a dear friend of my aunt Jessie. Now in her fifties, she had come to our home with a strange message from the Lord to share with aunt Jessie. She turned to my aunt and spoke, "I have a word from the Lord." Then she began to cry and broke down as she continued to speak. "Before the year is over God will take you home to be with Him!" As my aunt listened, she also broke down and cried. This was in 1987.

Then this servant of God sat down and said, "Let me tell you what happened. I was praying and last night the Lord gave me a vision…I saw this beautiful procession. Angels, so many of them, were taking part in such a fabulous procession to heaven. They were dancing and singing. I said to the Lord, 'this is so beautiful. Who is this person for which such a fabulous procession is conducted as a welcome to heaven?' The Lord said, 'You know her.' I asked, 'I know her?' Then the Lord allowed me to see who that person was and I saw you!"

"I asked the Lord, 'but why are you showing me this?' The Lord replied, 'This year I am going to take her home to be with me.' I said, 'Lord, she is such a wonderful person! We need her here so she can continue to influence people, the government and people in key positions in authority and in the schools, among the parents and teachers, among workers and the staff.'

The Lord responded, 'No, it is time for her to come home.' I cried through the entire night and then the Lord spoke to me again. 'I want you to go to her home tomorrow and tell her.' 'Lord, I cannot tell her! How can anyone go and tell another person something like this?' He said, 'you are my servant. Obey what I tell you!' So, this lady was in my aunt's home and in a very loving manner disclosed the contents of her heart.

Aunt Jessie broke down and they hugged each other and cried. Then my aunt got up out of her chair and said, "Well, that is fine. If God wants me to go home, then I am ready. It is the best thing that can happen to me." However, neither the woman of God nor my aunt disclosed this information to anyone. We were in the same house and only separated by a wall. I talked to her several times but she never gave me a clue as to what had happened.

However, I guessed what was going on when she used phrases like, "All that I had to do, I have done. My work is over." I would say, "But we need you! You're such an inspiration. People need you and God is still using you." She would respond, "Yes, but my time is over." Later on I realized she had paid up all the subscription fees to Christian organizations for the whole year and distributed her wealth so that everyone received some portion of what she owned. She helped people start small businesses, created some self-run enterprises and she bailed people out of loans and debts. She visited some of the places that were close to her heart, especially the home for lepers. She not only shared her life with them but she shared her resources and her time. She shared everything!

At the end of the year I received a phone call saying, "Your aunt has become ill here at the school. She is complaining of a splitting headache. Somebody in the family needs to come." I was the only person available so I rushed to the school, gently carried her out and placed her in the car and took her to the hospital. For several days she was in a coma with a massive hemorrhage and lay in bed as if she were dead. I knew that God was preparing our family for her death.

God "prepared" us for five days and then Aunt Jessie was gone, at rest with her Lord. As I reflected on this I asked myself, "What is the big deal about being famous in this world, to be known as leaders and as even servants of God? I want to be famous in heaven. I want to make Jesus famous on earth!" I thank God I have kept that end in sight. Everything we do today is done in the light of eternity. I was greatly motivated by my aunt. What an example! What a way to finish her life! She was welcomed into the eternal dwellings by God. What a blessing!

My Aunt Jessie made a tremendous impact on my life. She was somebody who was small in stature but huge in the sight of God. She was an amazing woman of God; Jessie Moses motivated me to live a life that is pleasing to God, to walk in humility and share resources with one goal: To make Jesus known in every possible manner.

How I wish she were alive today. How we miss her! Our family can never be the same because of her exemplary life, being the servant of the most High God. I thank the Lord and Jessie Moses for the profound influence she has had in my life. After her death her body was placed in a casket. We all came to pay our last respects, family members, teachers and staff of the school, leaders of the church as well as some dignitaries of the State. Outside there was a huge traffic jam. Just as they placed the lid on the casket and were ready to take her body to the cemetery, a bus loaded with people suddenly entered the premises. The people hurried off the bus and were running into the room, screaming, "Mummy, mummy!" Then they broke down and cried. No one knew why. Later we realized that they were lepers. They fell on her body and cried, "Who will love us like you did? Who do we have now?" It broke our hearts. Then we realized that while my aunt had held huge positions in our city, she had used her time and resources to spend time with lepers, dressing their wounds, bandaging their sores, and spending her personal resources on them. She would buy material and clothes in abundance, employing tailors to provide them with fresh clothes, while she shared the love of God with them. What a great life! What an inspiration! Thank you, Jesus, for Aunt Jessie Moses.

The Drowning

ONE OF THE THINGS I ENJOYED GROWING UP, WAS BE-
ing together with my dad's extended family. My grandmother
used to say, "God has given me four daughters. If He would
give me sons, I will make them the four pillars of the Church."
With tears in her eyes she took her only possession, a gold ring,
placed it in the offering bag and said, "Lord, this is the vow that
I make."

As she cried to God she knew He heard her prayer. She was
blessed with five sons! Each of them sang in the church choir
and served the Lord in their own special way - a truly amazing
family! One of the things that we enjoyed most was simply to
be together as a family. We could always find some excuse to
be together such as going to the beach or attending a cricket
match. Cricket is the number one sport in India. I have amazing
memories of how we watched cricket matches as a family. We
also enjoyed playing different games together. Every Saturday
we would leave early to be at the public swimming pool even
though not everyone knew how to swim.

One Saturday, we were swimming in one of the pools at
the sports arena. As we were enjoying ourselves, one of the
friends in the neighborhood began to swim to the 18-foot deep
end of the pool reserved for diving. He swam right into the
middle of that area and began to drown. My cousin Paul decided to help him by pushing his body up from underneath, so
he could catch a breath of air. Standing around we could not
see any trace of him. My cousin's friend who had accompanied
us that day, decided to help the two of them. Then I went in to
help. The only thing I remember was that somebody grabbed
me from underneath and pulled me down into the depths of
the water!

Afterwards people told us what had actually happened.
The four of us had sunk into the depths of the diving pit. All

the others screamed and yelled but no one dared to jump in and attempt to save anyone. Four swimming pools away there was a young man named Das. Das was a rickshaw puller. In India we have a tricycle, called a rickshaw, which can hold 8-10 school children cramped into the narrow seating space. Das would take us through the crazy streets of Madras to our school. Now he had become a lifeguard at the pools. Das came dashing into the pool and dove into the 18-feet section. In one quick move, he grabbed all four of us up and out of the pool. A huge crowd gathered as we regained consciousness. I saw hundreds of faces peeking down at me to see if I was dead or alive. For the next four days I experienced this horrible feeling of being pulled down into the depths of a dark pool. Since my stomach was full of the water I had swallowed in the pool, the effect of the chlorinated waters felt like a chemical was released from within me. Night after night I woke up in fear that I was drowning. Looking back, I cannot help but thank God. Through this ordinary man Das, God snatched me from the jaws of death. I thank God for Das and every time I think of him, I think of Jesus who saved me from sin. What an awesome plan God had for my life. I thank you, Lord Jesus.

This Is My Name

MY NAME IS SUNDARSINGH MOSES. I HAIL FROM THE southern part of the state of Tamil Nadu in South India. Growing up I was very upset with my parents because they had given me this strange name. Often people would ask me why I had a North Indian name but looked like a South Indian. Of course I had no answer to that question. I would in turn ask my parents why they gave me that name. Even though they tried very hard to explain their reason to me, it never made sense.

My great grandfather was a medical doctor and a pastor of a church. Indian church history boasts of some great names belonging to people who made Jesus famous during their lifetime. One of them was Sundar Singh who hailed from Punjab in Northern India. This is his story:

At a very young age Sundar was brought to a spiritual guru who taught him the Hindu scriptures. He was a very pious, soft-spoken and well-mannered boy. But while he was young his mother died. At that point this mild-natured boy suddenly became boisterous and mischievous. Together with his friends he ridiculed his teachers in the mission school in which he studied. He made fun of Christ and accused his teachers of trying to convert him to Christianity. One day Sundar was given a copy of the New Testament. Being very upset, he gathered his friends together, poked fun at the Christians, tore pages out of the New Testament and flung them into the fire. The news of this incident reached his father who was very upset with the strange behavior of his son. He reprimanded his son and said, "You don't have the right to destroy a religious book of people of another faith."

After these events Sundar became restless. He often thought of the things he had done and became withdrawn. At the age of fourteen he shut himself away in his room and prayed, "God, I don't know who you are, but if you do not grant me peace to-night, I will put an end to my life by placing my body across the railroad line that is beside my home." He knew that every day a train ran on that track at 4.30 a.m. But at around 2:00 a.m. that morning, Sundar was awakened by a bright light in his room. He then heard a voice, "Sundar! Sundar! Why are you perse-cuting me?" Sundar knew he had heard the voice of Jesus. An immense peace flooded his heart as he had a personal encoun-ter with the Lord Jesus Christ. Quickly he ran to his father and announced that he had become a Christian. His father thought he was confused and uttering nonsense, probably having had a dream. Little did he realize that his son would be so strong that nothing would deter him from his newfound faith.

As a teenager Sundar put on saffron clothes — a sign of a re-ligious leader in India — and set out barefoot on a cross-country mission to share his faith in Jesus Christ. Everywhere he went he suffered persecution. He was often beaten up for sharing his faith in Christ. He also had extraordinary experiences with the Lord Jesus Christ and taught extensively from the teachings of Jesus from the Sermon on the Mount. He had a profound in-fluence on the people of India. Many people all over the coun-try turned to Christ. During one of his visits to South India, my great grandfather was assigned the task of interpreting his messages into the local language. Sundar had such a profound influence on his life.

Since my grandmother wished that somebody in our fam-ily would have this name, my dad gave the name to me. For twenty-one long years, I struggled with this name. But on Oc-tober 13, 1983, I knew its significance after I surrendered my life to the Lord.

Because I have this name, I can easily initiate a conversation today with people from all walks of life and explain to them the salvation that is found in Jesus alone. It usually starts like this. "How come you have this name?" I respond by sharing the story of Sundar Singh and his conversion. Then I talk about my life and my conversion experience as well. This enables me to give them an opportunity to be won over to Christ. Again, I am reminded that by giving me this special name, God had a plan for my life. I sometimes feel my name itself is an evangelistic tool. Thank you, Jesus!

The Heavenly Vision

AS A NEW BELIEVER IN JESUS CHRIST, I HAD AN AMAZ-
ing dream. It was so incredible that I decided not to disclose it
to anyone. Perhaps I was too scared and frightened to let anyone know where I had been, what I had seen and what I had
heard. This is how it happened.

My aunt Jessie Moses took my cousin, Shanthi Moses, to
visit a godly woman, Alice Davis, to spend time in prayer. Since
there was no one around to drive them, I volunteered to help.
I waited at the entrance while my cousin and aunt went inside.
Soon a young person approached me saying, "Why are
you waiting outside? Why don't you come in too? You can join
us in prayer." Realizing that Alice was unwell and therefore
unavailable, I consented. So, this young lady who was in the
house was going to pray in Alice's place. I wondered if anything significant could possibly take place through a young
person who was only a substitute for this godly woman. But as
she began to pray it became apparent that while she might be
young, she walked with the Lord and was hearing from Him.
As a young person I was fascinated to see how God was
working through her life. After she had prayed for both my
aunt and my cousin, she asked me if she could pray for me as
well. I readily consented. As she prayed she said, "God has
a great purpose for your life. He has already made it known
to you. Did he not speak to you in a vision? You saw yourself
leading a group of people. As you were leading them, you saw
massive earthquakes split the ground from underneath their
feet. You saw huge fires break out from beneath too. You called
out to them saying, 'Do not look down. Do not be afraid. Have
faith in God.'

"As the earth opened up, people in large numbers were being swallowed up as the flames engulfed them. Many, how-

ever, chose to take you at your word. As a result they were being carried by an invisible power over and across the wide chasms below them. You were encouraging them to press on since you were nearing the destination. As you were moving forward with the group you saw yourself approaching a place bathed in light. Later on you could see the glittering streets.

"Then you beheld the entrance to the portals of the incredible place. You saw paved streets glittering like gold and leading on to a flight of stairs. Just ahead of them you saw a huge throne. Upon it was enthroned One like the Most High God. You saw His face radiant like the sun. His long flowing garments were dazzling white and there were flashes of thunder and lightning behind him. You could see His form, see the outline of the face like that of the sun and then you heard a deep and booming voice, the voice of God himself, *My son, I have called you to be my servant. Prepare a people for me.*"

When she narrated the dream, I was taken back. That was exactly what I had seen and heard. I was rendered utterly speechless. I just broke down and wept.

"Brother, is this true?" she asked me. "Why didn't you tell anyone about it?" I replied that I had kept it to myself because it overwhelmed me. I could not believe what I had seen and wondered if I could ever be such a person in whom the Lord could do something significant. I had lived a mediocre life, was not ambitious and was satisfied with the simple things of life. I knew I had lived my life like a wretched sinner. I had been an enemy of God for most of my life and lived in sin for so long. I said, "I do not know what it means to be a Servant of God. I can't speak well. I am not gifted. I don't have the talents and abilities to handle such a responsibility. I don't have what it takes to be a Servant of God." This young woman said to me, "But these things don't happen to just anyone. What has happened in your life is very precious. I really do not know you well, but this one thing I know, God has a very grand plan for your life".

My Aunt Jessie encouraged me a lot. "If there is anything I can do to help, I am here for you and will support your decision. It is a great honor to be the servant of the Lord. Serve Him while you are young. If you need me to talk about it with your parents, I would be glad to. I am really proud of you."

I thank God for the role she played in my life. This great heavenly vision has inspired me over the years and given me the delight and joy to be God's servant. It has provided me great strength and encouragement in difficult times when I have faced huge problems and discouragements in ministry. Praise the Lord!

The Divine Appointment

IN MY EARLY TWENTIES, ONE DAY I WENT TO CHURCH and met brother Gladstone Samuel, a senior member of our church. He said to me, "Son, what are you doing here?" I told him, "I am doing what we are supposed to do on a Sunday; go to church, fellowship with other believers, listen to God's word and grow in faith." He responded, "That's what everybody is doing in the church. Who will do what we are supposed to do outside of the church, apart from attending the worship service?"

I told him, "I don't know anything about ministry. If you want I can help you. I can take you to a place, but I can't be involved. I don't know the basics of ministry." So he said, "You come with me, and I'll teach you." I quickly responded by saying, "No, no, I can come and help you but I don't know anything about ministry." To that Gladstone Samuel said, "OK, you don't need to do anything but do come with me." I did not know what his plan was, but I decided to go. I took him on my motorcycle and went to a specific neighborhood I was familiar with. It was located near the institution where I had received my education.

When we arrived, Gladstone Samuel said to me, "This is what we are going to do! We will stand at the end of the street and tell people about the good news of salvation. Anyone who listens and cares to pay attention will be the ones that we would want to lead to Christ." He found a place and began to speak. There were some windows open and people passing by. I never thought that any good could come out of it. He began to speak, "Dear brothers and sisters, I have come to tell you the good news of Him who came into this world to die for sinners like you and me."

Samuel gave the gospel message. He told the bystanders, "If there is no one else in this world willing to forgive you the sins you have committed, I want to tell you that there is one person willing to do so. His name is Jesus. In fact, He not only listens to you, but He paid the price for your sins." I was utterly shocked to see how people walking by had stopped, listened and responded in prayer to the offer of salvation. I thought, "What a message and response he has evoked! What a simple way of leading people to the Lord!" The time was up and we had to move on.

Then Gladstone Samuel said something that I was not prepared for. He said, "At the next place you are going to do it." With hesitation I replied, "No! No! I don't know anything. I don't know anything. I can't speak!" He did not make it easy for me. "You say exactly what I said." So we argued back and forth and finally I succumbed to his pressure. "Alright," I said. I realized that if I were going to wait much longer, we would be there the whole night. So we went to the next street and I found a secure place. I was really trembling. "OK, I will stand here," I told him. I knew the whole ordeal would be over quickly. I stood there and repeated almost the same message he had preached earlier. I said, "I have been a sinner for so many years but I know what it means to be forgiven. You too can be forgiven!" As I shared, some people stopped and listened and some came to me for prayer. I was so surprised to know that what I had tried to convey actually made sense to people. When we were done I said, "Let's hurry." I wanted to leave that place before anyone else approached me.

Just as we were about to leave I saw a lady seated across the street. She was trying to get us to come over to her. I said to brother Samuel, "Uncle, somebody is calling you." He looked at me and answered, "No, no, she is pointing to you." I asked him to come along with me. So we both went across the street to her. The lady told me, "Tell me all that you have to tell me. Tell me, I am willing to listen." I looked at her perplexed and said, "I don't know what you are talking about." She said, "You have something to tell me, don't you?" I replied, "Tell you what? I don't know what you are talking about!"

"Let me tell you my story," she told us. "You see, I am married. I have no children and my husband is an alcoholic. Every night he comes home and beats me up. He extracts every bit of money I have. If he can't find money, he takes things from my house, sells them at throwaway prices and takes that money for another drink. That is who he is. This has been going on for some time. I don't know when things will really change. Last night he came home terribly drunk. He beat me up. He was so mad with me. He shouted, 'Give me this little plot of land that is registered in your name. If you are my wife, submit to me. Since I am your husband, give me that document! You are supposed to submit to your husband.' Listen, I told him, if I did not care about you, then I would not even have stayed in this marital relationship. I want you to know that I care about you. If I give this land document to you, you will not return home dead-drunk, you will return home dead! I cannot allow that to happen! But he saw no reason. He beat me even more. He placed his foot on my chest trying to choke me. I screamed and yelled but nobody came to rescue me."

She continued her story. "Let me tell you something about my husband. He is such a wicked man he even paid someone money to cast a spell on me. I experienced a spirit in the form of a snake enter my body. I know it because I can hear the hissing of a snake within me. Can you believe it? Let me tell you more. Last night, I came to the end of my rope. I was so upset, so angry and frustrated. I worship thousands of gods and goddesses. I screamed and cried to them for help. I didn't know if anyone of them heard my prayers. 'Is somebody willing to listen, willing to help?' I didn't know who was going to help. I said, 'If you are God, help me. I have come to the end of my rope and if you are not going to help me, I can't take it any longer.' While I went through these moments in the middle of the night, I saw a strange brightness outside my house. Since we don't have streetlights, I went out to investigate. I then saw this light coming from out of the sky.

"I lifted my eyes and my head upward to see. To my utter shock, I saw a man descending from the sky. I was terrified and perplexed! His face shone like the sun, his garments were dazzling and glowing with light. In his hand was a drawn sword. Who is this man coming down from the sky? As I was looking with wonder and amazement the man said to me, 'Don't harm yourself. For tomorrow, before the sun sets, a man will come and stand right in front of your house and speak. Wait for him and when he comes, call him over because he has answers to all your questions.'"

As you can imagine, I was stunned by the words of this woman. I shuddered with fear as tears rolled down my cheeks. "Who am I? And what is it I am doing in this world?" I thought I was just an ordinary person doing insignificant things. Now I realized that God in heaven ordained my steps. The words I speak, the insignificant things that I do are the very things that matter to God. In fact, God is using me! I wept as I realized that what I speak and share about Christ is more than a mere human effort, it is a divine appointment. To God these experiences matter! To think that God had led me to that place, on that day, at that particular time with a specific word to prevent a suicide and provide hope and salvation is truly incredible!

That day I learned that even the smallest thing I do for God is important to Him. If it is that important, then I want to do whatever I can for God. With renewed energy I spoke words of comfort to her, challenged her to believe in Christ and told her, "God will set you free from this demonic possession." We cried to God in prayer and instantaneously the power of the Holy Spirit came and exorcised her as we uttered the name of Jesus. She was delivered from her sin and saved by the grace of God!

The following week I was invited to a church in the same neighborhood. It was a rundown church. We went to the terrace where we swept the floor and tried to beautify it in every way possible. We placed a couple of boxes on top of each other to erect a temporary pulpit and I got ready to preach that morning. Before we started the service, we went to the neighborhood to invite people to come join us. Brother Gladstone announced "Is there anyone who wants to share a testimony before our brother brings God's word?" I saw a woman struggling to get into the church on the top floor. It was the same woman I had prayed for a few days ago.

She said, "I would like to say something." This woman told us how God had mysteriously intervened in her life. She related the story of the angel who appeared to her and told her what to do and how "ordinary" me had been there and how God used that whole process to save her. Then she said, "This is the first and the last time I plan to come to this church. I realize that my legs can no longer support my body as I am suffering with acute arthritis. I had to carry my body step by step to be here. Since God has done such a great miracle in my life I could not stay away but had to come and share my experience."

After I had preached the word of God, brother Gladstone said, "Since God did all these things through you, why don't you pray for her?" Again, I responded, "No! I can pray for minor ailments like headaches and stomachaches but not these big problems. I think you should handle this one." Brother Gladstone said, "No, she has come to faith through your sharing. You pray for her. God will listen to you too." So, he shut his eyes and bowed his head in prayer. I had no option but to pray. I have never forgotten that prayer. I remember, I cried more than I prayed. I said, "Lord, who am I to pray? Who am I to pray for her?" I cried out to God in prayer and I said, "In the name of Jesus! Arthritis, I rebuke you!" Later on we continued to pray for the other people in this small church.

The following month I was once again invited to speak at this church. During the time for sharing testimonies I saw the same woman coming forward. She said, "Last month, this young man prayed for me. When I went home I realized that I had no pain and no symptoms of my problem. I have forgotten what arthritis is all about anymore. I also realized that maybe God did this for a purpose. Since I am able to walk again, I think I need to share my testimony with others." Throughout that month she told us how she had led four other women to the Lord and brought them to the church. This humble beginning has continued to keep me on my knees ever since.

Ministry is not about what we do. Ministry is what God does and what He accomplishes through us. Paul wrote in the book of Galatians, *"For God, who was at work in the ministry of Peter as an apostle to the Jews, was also at work in my ministry as an apostle to the Gentiles...."* (Gal 2:8 NIV). I wrote in the margin of my Bible and made "God...at work in my life," a prayer. That's what I think should be the billboard—the advertisement—for every Christian, "God at work!"

The Revelation of Jesus

ISN'T IT WONDERFUL TO TALK ABOUT JESUS? ISN'T IT strange that the resurrected and living Lord Jesus Christ, worshipped by millions of people worldwide, remains unseen by His followers and worshippers?

When I came to know Jesus Christ as my personal Savior, I was such an excited Christian. I went about sharing my faith with people on the streets. I witnessed to everyone I met in the Madras Christian College where I was pursuing a Master's degree in Economics. I enjoyed my newfound faith and cherished my special relationship with Jesus Christ.

While I worked in the bank during the day, I waited eagerly for the evening to set in. It would give me an opportunity to visit the man of God, John Joseph, that God used to lead me to Jesus Christ. I enjoyed spending time with him. Brother John Joseph was only too happy to see me and guide me into deeper spiritual levels. Every day I invariably witnessed people coming to faith in Jesus Christ. Some were delivered of demon possession while others received healing in their bodies. Every day was an exciting day. I wished I could be like him someday and make a difference for someone every day of my life. I went out to meet him every evening and returned home after midnight.

Although my parents knew my whereabouts, they refrained from saying anything because they had witnessed such a dramatic change in me. They were happy for what had happened in my life. On returning home, I would read the Bible through the night. The Bible became such a motivating and inspirational book. I searched for all the promises, highlighted them and claimed them for my life. As I came to the New Testament section, I was fascinated to see the things that Jesus said and did. It seemed to me that brother John Joseph was doing what the Lord himself was doing. I wanted to follow John Joseph as he followed Jesus Christ.

It did not take long before I realized that the church was doing something entirely different. They were following unimportant things that Jesus never asked us to do. The church seemed to lack the vibrant life that only the Holy Spirit can provide. It seemed strange that I could not recall when I had heard a Sunday morning sermon on the Holy Spirit. Consumed with revelations from the Word of God and questions concerning the state of the church, I soon realized I had been reading well into the early hours of the morning. I do not remember how much sleep I had during those times. I prayed, "Lord, if you want me to be awake and in prayer, please wake me up." I would jump out of bed every morning and head to the terrace just above Jessie Moses' apartment. I did not know what time it was because it was still dark and the moon lit up the night sky. I had such an inexpressible joy in my life. I was in touch with the Ultimate Reality.

The joy I had was a divine gift. My heart was filled with pure love for God. I wanted to be with Him more than I wanted anything else in my life. I reveled in His love all the time. Only one thing caused my heart to be saddened — as I read the Bible and observed how people enjoyed the privilege of seeing Jesus, having Him in their homes, experiencing His awesome touch that revived the sick and raised the dead, made my heart yearn for similar things. Could I experience Jesus in a similar fashion? Had he changed? Had His power diminished? Had the Bible that clearly described Jesus as He is, changed?

Is He the same unchanging God who declared, *"I am the same yesterday, today and forever?"* Is He able to reveal Himself to me? Could I not see Him? I had heard the testimonies of people and other servants of God of their experiences of seeing Jesus. If this was possible in their lives, I was convinced it could happen in mine, too!

As a new believer, I did not want to let any opportunity to attend a meeting go by. I wanted to be there to know more and grow in the faith. At one such meeting, I saw the crowds gather together. It was such an excitement to see so many of my friends — with whom I had grown up — come to faith in Jesus Christ in such huge numbers, almost at the same time. Surely God was at work because there was so much excitement in the city of Chennai. As I entered the parking lot, I saw a friend and classmate of mine, Sunny Matthews. He came up to me all excited and said, "Sundar, do you know what happened to Mahboob Khan." I told him that I had heard that Mahboob Khan had come from an Islamic background and that I had heard his amazing testimony of how God captured his heart and changed his life. He continued, "And, did you hear the latest? Jesus appeared to Mahboob Khan." I was so excited to know about that, but deep within I was sad that I did not have the same experience. As we continued our conversation, Sunny reminded me that the meeting was about to begin. I told him, "You run along. In a short while I will catch up with you."

When Sunny left, I burst into tears. I imagined what a privilege it must have been for Mahboob to see Jesus. I said, "Lord, I am so excited and happy for what you have done for Mahboob Khan but would you appear to me as well? Could I ever see you? You know how I long to see you." As the meeting got underway, I knew my heart was no longer there. My heart was drawn to something bigger than what was preached there. I rushed home. When I arrived, I slammed the door and collapsed on the bed, again bursting into tears. I was intensely searching for Jesus and cried out to God from the depth of my being, a cry of desperation. "If you are God and the Savior of my soul, allow me the privilege to see you." I knew that He would never be partial or show favoritism. I reminded God of what He had declared in His word. I pointed out to God from Jeremiah 29:13, "*You will seek me and find me when you seek me with all your heart.*" I looked at several other passages of scripture to strengthen my case before God. I read and reread passages from the scripture telling of people who saw the Lord. I imagined the joy and excitement they must have experienced. I concluded that what God said in His word could not be altered. I knew God was always true to His character. I became more and more confident that Jesus would appear to me. It was only going to be a matter of time. So I knelt down and made it a prayer. I continued to pray until it became the passion of my life.

One day I felt the Lord asking me, "Sundar, if this is so important to you, then why is this request just one of the items on your prayer list?" I realized I had been so foolish. As a result I prioritized this request and made it the foremost item on my prayer list. The first thing that I prayed would be the most important request I had. It was simple. I wanted to see Jesus.

After several weeks of praying it occurred to me that I was still wrong somewhere. If this was important, how could I allow other things to crowd my prayer list? I removed every other item, no matter how important they seemed. My prayer list had only one request—I want to see Jesus! I waited on the Lord and sat through the night. When I dozed off, I found myself jumping out of bed fearing that Jesus might have come and gone and found me sleeping! I shed tears as I sang, worshipped and prayed through the nights.

Many times friends at work noticed the redness in my eyes. They suspected that I had some problem. I told them how excited I was! I told them I was in pursuit of God. I continued to fast and pray. I fell prostrate on the floor many a night. Nothing seemed to happen. Six months had gone by but even though I was disappointed and physically exhausted, I was determined and unwilling to give up.

While reading the Bible, I came across a passage from the Sermon on the Mount. *"Blessed are the pure in heart, for they will see God"*(Matt. 5:8 NIV). Wow! I get it! Now I know why Jesus had not appeared to me, I thought. I am not pure in heart. I would never be. I wept with much sadness. I said, "Lord, how foolish of me to pray a prayer when the truth is so clearly expressed in the scripture. Lord, I am really sorry for praying such a prayer. Forgive me, Lord. But, I still want to see you!" I prayed again that night.

As usual, early the next morning, I went up to pray. When the sun came up, I flipped through the pages of scripture. My eyes fell on a passage from the gospel of John 14:18 (NIV), *"I will not leave you as orphans; I will come to you."* I felt as though the words jumped right out of the Book. I burst out in praise and thanksgiving to the Lord. It was the first week in February 1985.

That afternoon, I decided to catch a short nap. As I lay in bed I pondered the things that were going on in my life. Suddenly my little room began to be bathed in pure light. Jesus himself was standing in front of me! His clothes were dazzling with brilliant light. His face was glowing like the sun. I could not see distinct features or His long flowing hair. He turned His face toward me. I experienced strange beams of light flowing forth from His eyes and filling my heart with inexpressible love and peace. My heart seemed to explode. His love could not be contained in a human heart. The feeling is difficult to put into words. I cried out, "Jesus! Jesus! Jesus!" In response, Jesus smiled back at me. Then the whole room was bathed with light of a greater intensity. By this time, it was impossible to behold His face any longer. I cried out, "Lord, I can't see you." I could not contain the love, joy and peace that flooded my heart. I desperately wanted to run and invite everyone to come and see the Jesus I always desired to see.

At the same time, I feared He might leave before I returned. I wondered if this was the return of Christ! It was then that a cloud seemed to come in between us. I regained my sight but I could not see Jesus any longer. I burst out in tears again. I desired to see Him again. That cloud lifted and once more I saw the face of Jesus. He had His familiar smile. This time around, He raised His hands to bless me and then He was gone.

I have cherished every moment of that experience ever since. I will never forget what I saw and how I felt. What an awesome Jesus! That day I knew the meaning of the scripture passage found in Jeremiah 29:13 (NIV). *"You will seek me and find me when you seek me with all your heart."*

I thank you, Jesus, for this great revelation of who you are. Thank you.

The Lame Walk

IN THE LATE EIGHTIES I HAD THE PRIVILEGE TO BE PART of what God was doing in our church in the city of Chennai, South India. We had a fantastic pastor at the church, Rev. Dr. Martin Alphonse. He encouraged us to engage in evangelism and created excitement in the church. Because of his invitation, I became part of the excitement of the church.

With a view to plant churches, we often went as teams to different villages to preach the gospel. I was a member of one team which went to another town about 3 ½ hours from the city of Chennai, known for a famous Christian hospital.

When we arrived there, we stopped just outside of the hospital. I was probably the youngest member of this evangelistic team. Regardless, I had to carry my share of responsibility. We took turns preaching in the different villages so that people would be lead to Christ. The leader of the team was Pastor Francis Selvan, a dynamic leader and a man of God. He was also a man of prayer and the Word. He was such an enthusiastic individual. I felt blessed to be associated with him and we became great friends.

That first morning, while the team was getting ready, Pastor Selvan suddenly announced to the group, "Now Brother Sundar Moses will share something." Startled I asked, "What am I supposed to do?" He had caught me off guard. Pastor Selvan responded, "Share what is in your heart." I was not prepared so I said, "Let us sing a couple of songs." This gave me a few moments to flip through my Bible where my eyes fell on Matthew 9:35. *"Jesus went through all the towns and villages, teaching in their synagogues, preaching the good news of the kingdom and healing every disease and sickness."*

I started, "We have come here to preach the gospel. I believe we have forgotten to do all that Jesus did. He went about preaching, healing and delivering all those who were oppressed. We must do the same. Some aspects of ministry have been lost in Christian ministry. You see if you are a Christian, God wants you to have a doctorate in His University. P stands for preaching, H stands for healing and D stands for delivering people who are demon possessed. Every disciple needs to have a PhD. Don't be afraid of people. Let's go, preach and pray. It is not about us, it is about Jesus. He will do the miracles. He has not changed one bit."

As I finished, Pastor Selvan came and hugged me in front of everybody. He was so excited. He said, "The Lord has spoken through this man this morning and I want to encourage you. We will have many opportunities to preach but we must also take time to pray for miracles."

So, we gathered together, prayed and set out for the day. I recall that in a particular village one of the team members was preaching the gospel and leading people to Christ. Pastor Selvan came up to me and asked, "Brother Sundar, what are you doing here?" I said, "Well, I am just wondering what Jesus would be thinking about us and what we are doing. What do you think He would be thinking?" Pastor Selvan replied, "WOW! That's an interesting observation."

As we were talking and pondering these questions, the team members called out for us to come so that "we could get to other villages." But, as we were about to leave, a man—probably in his mid-70's—came up to us. He was dragging his body and using a stick to support himself. He held out his hands to us. It was obvious that he wanted something. That day I realized, what it means to have the compassion of Christ. For reasons unknown to us, this man's poor physical condition caused us to break down. He looked so helpless. We wished we could do something for him. Pastor Selvan asked him what we could do for him. The elderly gentleman said, "You have been speaking about this Jesus. Can He do something for me?" "Like what?" I asked. He replied, "I want to be well."

The old man shared his story with us. "I was a member of the Indian Army that fought in the India-Pakistan war in 1971. Look at me now! I am retired and I am paralyzed. Half of my body has lost its sensitivity. I have been bedridden for years, but when I heard these things, I somehow dragged my body here. Can your Jesus do something for me?" I wanted to run away. Did I want to pray for a man who is paralyzed? No way! It's so easy to preach but so challenging to practice what we preach! Grabbing me by the hand, Pastor Selvan reminded me that God had spoken through me that very morning. "Let's pray for a miracle," he said. "Sure, let's pray!" I replied.

Thank God for Pastor Selvan who encouraged me to pray that day! "Sundar you do one thing, you pray for his upper body, waist up, and I will pray for his lower body, waist down," he said. "When we have finished praying, we will turn him around and together we must shout aloud, 'In the name of Jesus, walk!' Then we will just let him go." "Huh?" I said, "Oh yes, sure." One part of me was terrified but I was also excited. Pastor Selvan took the stick the man was leaning on. The man could hardly balance or stand. We told him, "Before we pray for you, believe that Jesus will do this work for you." He immediately responded with, "Yes! Of course!"

Then I began to pray for his arms, for his joints, neck, vertebrate, spine and whatever came to my mind that was "waist up." Pastor Selvan was praying for his hips, knees, his ankles and feet. We prayed. We wept. Then we turned him around. We screamed at the top of our voices, "In the name of Jesus, WALK!" I don't know what Pastor Selvan did but I know what I did. I closed my eyes! There was such silence. Such silence. I put my hands in front of my face. I did not have the courage to look. What a moment!

After what seemed a long time, I separated my fingers and I peeped through them. To my utter amazement, the man had already walked fifteen yards away from where he had been. He was walking! Our hearts burst with joy. We hugged each other, cried and then Pastor Selvan shouted to him, "Is this the way to walk? Remember, you were an officer in the Indian Army. Walk like an army officer!" The man swung his arms and thighs as high as he could and he walked shouting out loud, "Left right!; Left right!"

As he was walking back to his village, people began to gather around him. The other team members jumped off their vehicles and joined in the excitement. We explained, "This man was paralyzed but now he is walking as we prayed in Jesus' name. Here in our hands is his walking stick." As the crowds swelled we walked along with him back to the village. The people came out of their houses shaking their heads in disbelief.

We asked, "Who do you think made this man well?" They replied, "Jesus!" We stopped at the end of the street and said, "Believe in Jesus. He is such an amazing God who loves you. He cares for you. He died on the cross for you."

As the celebration continued, the excitement remained with us and we preached another sermon to the people. Over 70 of them gave their lives to the Lord. They knelt down in the street and with tears running down their cheeks they received Jesus Christ as their personal Savior. Later on I came to know that Pastor Selvan established a church there since the gospel had never been preached in that place before. PRAISE THE LORD! JESUS, THANK YOU FOR THE MIRACLE.

My Dream Girl

MY WIFE AND I COME FROM THE SAME CHURCH, THE Emmanuel Methodist Church in Chennai in South India. Since my dad and Angie's mom were members of the youth fellowship many years ago our families knew each other well. In fact, the day Angie was born, my parents had visited the hospital. Angie was well known in the church as an active member of the junior choir. She also held a leadership role in the youth fellowship, was part of the "JAS" trio, member of the senior choir and was a Sunday school teacher. By virtue of being a youth leader, Angie was a member of the official Board of the church of which my dad was a long-standing member.

In conversation one day, my dad mentioned that he had three children. Angie told my dad that she did not know the third child but was familiar with both my older sister and younger brother. She immediately came over to question me as to why we had not met before. I was in the middle of a conversation with my own circle of friends at that time and felt embarrassed. I told her that we had not met because I was rare! That was our first meeting. I went home thinking how different she was from me: I was reserved and she was so friendly and sociable.

During that time, I woke up one day after a strange dream. I was shocked to see my own wedding ceremony taking place in a church. I wondered why I was having a dream about my own wedding? I was not ready for marriage. In fact, I wanted to stay out of the marriage scene. It was then that the Lord said to me, "My son, recall the dream, for the girl you have seen in your dream is the one you will marry!" Like the apostle Peter, I began to protest. "No, Lord! She is so different when compared to me." I recognized both the church and the place where the wedding reception was taking place. I was confused. All the wedding receptions in our extended families had taken place on the premises of the school headed by my Aunt Jessie. This place looked different. As months rolled by, I set the dream aside, but God had other plans.

The speaker in a youth camp backed out at the last minute. The organizer sent someone to ask me if I could fill in. When I returned from work, I saw a person waiting at home with plans to take me as the last minute replacement. I tried to excuse myself. But, as usual, God had other plans. I left for the camp that very night.

Early the next morning I got up to be in prayer. As I walked around the campus praying I saw Angie in the distance. She was beside an open well helping draw water for the kids in the camp. I kept wondering if she was the same person I had observed in the church. Perhaps she is simple, I thought, a down to earth kind after all. During the night the leaders of the camp met for a review meeting. I was invited to join them. They took turns sharing their personal testimonies. I was also asked to share.

It was during the sharing of my testimony that the Lord started to speak to Angie about me. Later on Angie reminded me of what I had shared at the meeting. I had told them that although I was working in the bank, "I have a burning desire to serve the Lord. I am waiting for the right time to move into full-time ministry." Angie had desired to go to seminary right after her schooling, but she was not allowed to. So she pursued a degree in Physics. When she was not permitted to go to seminary after that degree, she enrolled for a Masters in Electronics. When her desire was not fulfilled again, she did another Masters in Nuclear Physics. Her student life became so extended. Someone advised her that the only way she could serve the Lord was if she married a person with a similar desire. So, Angie began to pray over the matter specifically.

Meanwhile my parents were pressuring me to get married. In India most marriages are arranged. The parents find suitable life partners for their children. The children in turn trust their parents' judgment. They thought Angie would make a great life partner for their son. I maintained my silence, as the two families could not come to an agreement immediately. I did not know what the real issues were. But I felt a sense of rejection and real hurt. The Lord spoke to me from Hab. 2:3 (NIV). *"For the revelation awaits an appointed time; it speaks of the end and will not prove false. Though it linger, wait for it; it will certainly come and will not delay."* I was not sure if I was correctly interpreting this scripture. I wrote down my dream. I knew things would happen but not without a delay. I told my parents not to bother me with other proposals. The arrangements were delayed for 1½ years. Meanwhile, two significant things happened.

First, my father had accompanied a man of God, Pastor James, to minister in another city. When the meetings were over, Pastor James asked my dad if he had any prayer requests. My dad wanted him to pray about his son's marriage. Pastor James replied, "Brother Moses, this thing does not need prayer! If you have anything else in your heart, kindly let me know." My dad was shocked. He thought to himself, "Here I am, anxious about my son's marriage that has been delayed, while this man seems so insensitive to the whole thing." My father wanted to clarify the situation. Pastor James told my dad, "Brother Moses, the Lord tells me that the girl's father will soon approach you to arrange for their marriage!" My dad could not believe his ears. On returning he told every word of the conversation to the family. Pastor James often called my dad to find out if what he had predicted had taken place.

The second significant thing involved my visit to see Annie Johnson. Throughout my formative years I was greatly influenced by a godly woman, Annie Johnson. She walked with the Lord in such close intimacy, the likes of which I had rarely seen in my life. Feeling so discouraged, I decided to pay her a visit one evening. As I shared with her, she prayed with tears falling from her eyes. During the prayer she said, "This is what the Lord says, 'My son, you have waited patiently. But my time has come. I will do that which I have promised. My time has come! Now it will take place.'" I looked at my wristwatch, just in case. Filled with joy and expectation, I returned home. As I eagerly waited outside our home, I saw my dad returning home late in the night after a church meeting. He was filled with joy. He gathered the family and told them what had happened that night. At the exact moment that I was in prayer with Annie Johnson, Angie's dad had approached my father and told him that without delay the marriage must take place!

Shortly after this incident Angie and I were married in the very church and in the very venue for the wedding reception that I had seen in my dream! Later on I was told that the venue where the wedding reception took place had been an empty piece of land when I had the dream. When God showed it to me in a dream, no one had even conceived the idea of the building in their heads!

I married the girl of my dreams!

The Book to Be Read

I AM EXCITED FOR THE CHRISTIAN HERITAGE THAT I have, not in terms of the numbers of years we have been Christians or our families have known Christ, but the meaningful experiences and encounters we can have when we live for the Lord Jesus Christ. As much as I talk about myself, I am so amazed to see how God has worked in my dear Angie's family as well.

Angie's maternal great grandfather served as a Hindu temple priest. A temple priest in India is a position of great influence in his village. Across from the village a river ran by. One day a white man came riding on a horse and tried to cross the river in order to get to his village. As the temple priest, Angie's great grandfather gathered the people together and encouraged them to defend the village. They pelted stones on the white man who was attempting to cross the river. The people of the village continued doing this for some time. One night while the priest was sitting outside his temple, he saw a mysterious man appear in the sky. His face was shining and his clothes were dazzling with light. He had a drawn sword in his hand. As he descended from the sky, the priest looked at him in wonder and amazement, for he had never seen anyone like this man before. He was terrified. This mysterious stranger looked at him and said, "Read the book! Read the book!" Then he disappeared into the sky.

The priest was perplexed. Who can I share my experience with, he wondered. Who will believe me? What will they think of me? I am the religious head here. I am the one who provides the answers to the questions the villagers have. How can I tell them about my experience? So he kept it in his heart and pondered over it. One day the white man made another attempt to cross the river to get to the village.

This time the priest asked the villagers to let the man cross the river and come into the village. Then he said to the man, "Why do you want to come into our village when we have made it obvious to you that you are not wanted in this place?" The white man responded, "It is because I desire to share some good news with you." The priest said, "What good news? Tell me now." The white man said, "But I need some time." The priest asked, "Why do you need time?" The white man replied, "Because it is in a book!" The minute he said "book," the priest said, "Alright, tell me what is in that book."

The white man took the Bible and shared with him about the good news of Jesus Christ who gave his life for sinners so he could be saved. The priest immediately received Jesus Christ as the Lord of his life. He quit his profession, his temple and left the village. He followed the white man. Later on he became an outstanding evangelist. Walking barefoot, he covered village after village. In his lifetime, he shared the gospel and led hundreds of people to Jesus Christ.

One day, Angie's great grandfather shared his heart's desire with some people. "I desire to die preaching the gospel and telling about my Savior, the Lord Jesus Christ." God answered that prayer too! As he was preaching in a church one day he suddenly clasped his chest, his body slumped to the floor and he was gone. Not a person shed a tear since they knew his end was nothing but an answer to his prayer. He lived such a noble life.

I thank God for the glorious heritage that I have from my wife's family. Thank you Lord.

Part II

ANSWERING GOD'S CALL

One of the Least of
These Brothers Of Mine

IN 1990, THE PASTOR OF THE EMMANUEL METHODIST Church, Rev. Dr. Martin Alphonse, asked me to take the role of Youth Advisor for the Methodist Youth Fellowship. He said to me that he was hearing reports of my involvement in other ministries. He wanted me to get involved in the activities of the church.

I was reluctant to accept. I did not want to get involved in church activities. I chose to be a silent and unknown member of the church. But, Pastor Martin Alphonse insisted. He said that if I did not voluntarily take up the responsibility, he would simply announce my appointment during a church service! I was furious inside. Finally, I succumbed to his pressure. My wife, Angie, was completely dedicated to the ministry of the church, but I was just the opposite. God must surely have had a great sense of humor in joining the two of us together as husband and wife.

While I was grumbling, Angie seemed to be highly excited with the opportunity for ministry. With her encouragement and support, I gradually became involved. During this time, we had some fabulous opportunities to work with the youth. The first thing I did was to get to know them. That meant giving them time. Soon my wife and I found ourselves in church every evening after work.

I played soccer with them while she spent time talking to them individually. The interactions enabled us to share our experiences with them. We ended the day with singing and prayer. Many in the fellowship brought their non-Christian friends to the church. These kids were interested in playing soccer. The number of young people in the fellowship grew to more than 50! We were now having problems managing the growing numbers. Soon there was a shortage of space too. These issues were problems but they were good problems.

The abundant talent and enthusiasm of the young people, coupled with a commitment to follow Jesus Christ, resulted in some fabulous concerts. It combined individual and group singing, skits and choreography and a short powerful message from the pastor. The experience was awesome. Along with this, we visited homes, hospitals, orphanages, institutions for the mentally challenged, preached in the slums and outreach centers, produced radio programs and periodically conducted all-night prayers, retreats and camps. Many of the young people gave their lives to the Lord as a result of this ministry.

During one Christmas season, we were invited to do a television program for a leading Christian organization. It resulted in a whole day of shooting in a professional outdoor studio. The youth thoroughly enjoyed the experience. The program was a Christmas play depicting people who were desirous of seeing Jesus. The theme was from the teaching of Jesus in Matthew 25:40 (NIV), *"The King will reply, 'I tell you the truth, whatever you did for one of the least of these brothers of mine, you did for me.' "*

A few days later, my wife was at home disposing of some unwanted stuff that had been lying around. A poor lady had come to our home to collect the articles. While this was going on, Angie was prompted to give something to the woman as a Christmas gift. She went in and brought out a new white saree, a traditional Indian dress, and gave it to her. The minute the woman received it from my wife she put down her bags, stood up and filled with the Spirit broke into praise. She loudly began to worship the Lord and thank Him for having answered her prayers. It was then that we came to know that she was a Christian and had prayed to the Lord, asking Him to provide her a new white saree so she could attend the worship service on Christmas day. Now the Lord had answered her prayers. While she praised the Lord spontaneously, she also blessed our family.

David, our son, had been playing in the room and burst out saying, "Daddy! Daddy! Come in and see. Jesus is walking by!" Praise the Lord. God opened the eyes of our son, David, to enable him to see Jesus walking right through our home.

In that moment, I knew that the play that was enacted for the television program was something that honored the Lord. When we had done something for the least of the ones in the family of God, Jesus himself arrived at our home! You will surely agree with me that it was the best Christmas anyone could ever wish for.

As I Look Outside My Window

I STARTED MY BANKING CAREER IN 1984. THE DEAD-line to accept the appointment was February 17. However, my study program was not concluding until the end of May. I could not make a decision. I had a dilemma as to whether I should complete my studies or get to work. I fasted and prayed.

Brother John Joseph helped me immensely. He told me that I needed to take up the job and the Lord would call me into full time service at a later time. From the very first day I did not like to be where I was. I made great friends at my work place and enjoyed what I was doing, but deep within me I knew I was in the wrong place. Was I going to do this all my life? Was there a more meaningful and satisfying job for me to do? What about the vision I had seen? I knew I was not going to be a banker like my Dad all my life. I knew God had chosen me to be his servant.

At times I felt confused. At other times, I felt excitement over the possibilities that could take place. I shared my feelings with my friends at work. They told me they too suffered great frustration through the monotony of work. They too wanted to quit but could not find alternatives. They told me that I would be all right after a period of time. They told me not to be hasty in making any decisions. I knew that they could not understand the spiritual quest within. I did not wish to be misunderstood since I was the only Christian in my bank.

Meanwhile, I knew I was not ready for any ministry God had for my life. In fact, I did not even know what that ministry was at that moment. I did not even know the basics. It turned out that the next ten years in the Bank was a time of exposure and training to do the Lord's work. I decided to make use of every opportunity to learn something. I was actively involved in different ministries as a volunteer. From 1983 to 1987, I served with brother John Joseph. From 1987 to 1989, I was a volunteer with a missionary organization under the guidance of brother Ashok. From 1990 to 1994, I was with the Emmanuel Methodist Church where Rev. Martin Alphonse became my mentor and pastor. Almost ten years had quickly passed by.

One evening after I returned home after a day's work at the bank, Angie made me a cup of tea. I was sitting by the window overlooking the street. As I watched all the people walking by, I asked myself these questions. "Where are these people going? Do they know the Jesus I know? If I do not let them know, then who else will?" I felt so selfish and satisfied. I wondered if I really cared about anyone. The questions seemed to haunt me. I felt I needed to do something. It was then that I received these inspirational words from the Lord. I woke up in the middle of the night, pulled out a piece of paper and wrote down the words the Lord had given me.

As I look Outside My Window

As I look outside my window
And I see all the people passing by
I stop and wonder if they ever know
That my Jesus died upon a gruesome cross
Was betrayed, denied, despised, crucified
And through His great redemptive sacrifice
He might save all humankind

Chorus
O, how will they ever know?
That my Jesus loves them so
Until people like you and I
Redeemed and to sin have died
Committed, unashamed to preach Jesus Christ

God turned these meaningful words into a song. I could not stop singing the song. Often it brought tears to my eyes. Many evenings I sat by the window, sipped coffee and began to sing this song. After several such days, I felt God speaking to me through the song I had sung. I felt constrained to do something about it. It was only a matter of time until I made the decision, a decision that I would never regret. It meant taking risks against the tide of life and embarking on the greatest adventure of all. As I look back, I thank God for the journey. It happened one evening as I sat by the window looking out.

The Cost of Discipleship

THE YEAR WAS 1994. BY THIS TIME I HAD WORKED 10 years at the bank. Every day was a day of reckoning with the purpose of my life. I had so many questions.

"What should I do with my life? Do I have to sit here and count the money belonging to other people? Do I need to process the papers so that people can take loans to further their financial positions? Should I handle all the personal requests and desires for free time so that others can plan their holidays and have privileges? Should I be involved in all these things that pertain to a temporary world?"

I had come to know the God of eternity. I felt strangely disturbed. I enjoyed the friends at work, the responsibilities, the challenges and the security of holding a Government job. I was married to a great wife, Angie. I lived in a new apartment close to my parents. I was involved in church activities. I did several things outside the church too. Why did I feel disturbed? Could it be that the God who provides us peace also could cause this disturbance? I did not know the answers. Every day the questions seemed to assault me. Was I in the right place? Was I doing the right thing? Deep in my heart I knew I wasn't. God had other plans, bigger than what I could perceive in my head. I knew it in my heart. I knew I had to wait for his timing. Ten years had gone by. I could not bear the frustration any longer. I was forced to pray like this. "Lord, if you want me to continue with the banking career, remove this frustration. If not, intensify it! May I never be able to go to work!"

I knew God loves radical praying! He heard my prayer and answered it. Strangely, I found it difficult to motivate myself to go to work. Sometimes, I left for work but half way there I decided to return home. At other times, I could just not get out of the house. I realized it was time to say goodbye to my friends and work and move on. God had answered my prayer. I was unable to get to work!

A tree falling down into our driveway had to be cut down. As I saw it lying there, the Lord reminded me that I was like that tree. I had been cut down, but the stump remained. It could grow all over again. A few days later some men came to uproot the whole tree. I knew that was what the Lord wanted me to do.

By this time we were into the fourth year of our marriage. Since I was struggling, I asked Angie for some advice. "What do you think I need to do?" I asked her. She told me that the best thing for me to do was to obey the Lord. "What is He telling you to do?" she asked. I told her that God wanted me to leave the bank and serve Him full time. She told me to simply obey. "God will take care of our family."

I thanked God for a woman who loves the Lord. I admired her simplicity, faith and encouragement. What a great gift God had given to me! After all, she was God's choice! Every day I thank God for giving me Angie.

Then I shared my concerns with Rev. Martin Alphonse. He encouraged me to spend time in prayer. We met over the next 18 months. Looking back, I am amazed how such a great man of God had time to help and guide my life. Surely he must have had many other responsibilities. As we sat by the seaside and retreat centers, he shared his journey of life with me. He encouraged me to take a step of faith. He shared the miracles God had done in his life and in his family. It brought great encouragement and excitement. I wondered whether these things could happen in my life as well. It was time to step outside the boat. It was time to take a step of faith. There must be something in that step! There must be something outside the boat. I wanted to be a risk-taker! I wanted to be a Peter!

On June 20, 1994 it was time to take that first step of faith. My boss was shocked to see my resignation letter on his table first thing in the morning. He told me I was doing a foolish thing. He insisted that he would not act on my resignation until I brought my wife to the bank. Soon she arrived at his office. On seeing her in an advanced stage of pregnancy, he thought she was out of her mind too. My wife calmly explained the rationale behind our decision. As I walked out of the bank I felt like a bird that had been set free from the cage - free to serve the Lord.

My parents, as well as Angie's parents, were anxious about our decision. Pastor Martin encouraged me to pursue a theological degree because it would open doors of opportunity for ministry. He also wanted me to study abroad and told me it would come in handy if I was considering pastoral ministry.

I was not convinced about any option he had put forth. I had given some personal requests to God. I did not want to go to seminary. I did not want to go into full time ministry. I did not want to depend on others for my financial support. I did not want to go abroad. I was willing to be involved in any ministry except pastoral ministry! All of them were turned down! So much for knowing how to pray! Maybe I could teach people how not to pray.

Pastor Martin pressured me to get the applications for pursuing theological studies. I ended up applying to Fuller Seminary, Trinity Evangelical Divinity School and Trinity Theological College in Singapore. I even applied to a college in India. I believe that was good enough for me. I was not a very ambitious person. That same year the bible college in India experienced some internal problems, so I was forced to drop the option of studying in India. Pastor Martin encouraged me to go ahead with the other options. Every time I saw him he reminded me to complete the forms and send them to the other schools. I had no clue where to begin. I found it easier to fill in all categories on the forms except for the section concerning finances. I prayed and committed the process to God.

Pastor Martin insisted that I not let the deadline for submitting the applications pass by. One day he asked me what God was telling me to do. I told him that God assured me that He would supply all my needs. I quoted Ephesians 3:20 (NIV). It became a promise for that particular moment. *"God is able to do immeasurably more than we can ask, think or imagine according to his glorious riches."* Wow!! I was so grateful to God.

I still had not submitted the forms. Pastor Martin asked me to write what the Lord had told me. So, I bought a good marker pen and across the financial status I wrote Ephesians 3:20. I was relieved because I believed my application would be turned down. My story would be over. It was better not to take the risk and upset a secure life. I wished that nothing positive would happen. I could even blame God for not doing anything on my behalf. Such crazy thoughts ran through my mind. It was a spiritual way of shelving something that was God's will.

To my wonder and amazement, I was accepted in all three educational institutions. They were interested in me! They were even willing to provide partial scholarships for me! There were provisions to help students coming from a third world country!

Once again, I felt excitement about the possibilities and fear over the uncertainty that loomed in front of me. I was disappointed because costs were high and resources negligible. Pastor Martin advised me to consider Singapore as an option. It could be advantageous because it was closer to home and would give me exposure to a cross-cultural setting, especially if God called me to be a cross-cultural missionary.

While reading the Bible I came across a passage in which Jesus told a rich man, *"If you want to follow me, go and sell all your possessions, give it to the poor, then come and follow me."* I remembered all the rich men who needed to hear the word of the Lord. I never could imagine that this passage would challenge my personal life. Anyway, I felt it was unreasonable for Jesus to make such a steep offer. Why did Jesus make it so difficult for this man or anyone else who desired to follow Him? I meditated over the passage again and realized that Jesus would never ask anyone to do anything that He did not do Himself. He had left the riches of heaven to stand before this man. The rich man could not respond properly because he did not have a sufficient revelation of Jesus Christ. The problem with our obedience is not about our appropriate response, it is with our inadequate revelation of Jesus Christ. It is an adequate revelation that will determine our appropriate response. I protested, "Lord, I am not a rich man. I am not that rich man. You know my bank balances. You know I am quite happy to be where I am." The Lord said to me, "Sundar, if you really trust me, then sell everything and follow me. Anything that does not allow you to obey me and do my will and live out my purpose is your riches. It is not about money. It is about anything that stands between you and me."

I shed many tears as these words broke my heart. I shared what the Lord had said to me with Angie. Her response? "If that is what God is telling you, let us sell everything and follow him." I did not expect that response from her. I thought my wife was supposed to be on my side but Angie was on God's side. And, in the end, we decided to do what God wanted.

We prayerfully put an advertisement in the newspaper that read: All household articles for sale! We sold everything. By that time, we had been married for about four years. Some of the wedding gifts we had received were not even opened. We were so excited following Christ that we did not take time to think about these unopened gifts. A colleague from the bank where I had worked earlier came to our home to buy something, not knowing that it was my residence. He told me he could not take anything from me so I explained the reason why we were selling our personal belongings. It took us two to three weeks to dispose of everything. The furniture, the appliances and other things were sold one by one. As my dad watched the items leave the house he looked really concerned even though he knew we were doing this because God had made it clear that this was what He wanted.

Soon the word spread that Sundar was out of his mind. They were talking about how I was selling things, how I had quit my job. They were not sure if I had really found God's will for my life. It was the talk of the town. Angie was now expecting our second child, Esther. Our son David was two-years old by now. Angie was almost eight months pregnant. People told me that I was crazy. We decided that Angie would go back to her parents' home while I left for school in Singapore. I bid her goodbye, received a visitor's visa and went off to Singapore not knowing what lay ahead of me.

After I reached Singapore my whole world came crashing down. I suddenly found myself struggling. I was alone. Every possible doubt assaulted me. Where have I come to? What have I done? Turning back was not an option. I spent the nights praying as tears flowed from my eyes. I learned it was better to be empty in the will of God than to have plenty outside of God's will. That is the kind of environment that often produces the resources of heaven to come down upon God's servants. It was a time that caused me to count the cost. And, it was then that God put a song in my heart.

A Mustard Seed

When everything seems to close down upon your life
Don't forget to lift up your head and look up with your eyes

Then you will soon realize, Jesus standing by your side
With his hands stretched out and his arms open wide

Chorus
What you need today is a mustard seed of faith
And as you exercise it, all your mountains will fade away
Then you will know my friend, that what Jesus said He will do
What He's done for me, He will certainly do for you.

When God Provides Through the Ravens

IT WAS THE FIRST WEEK OF JULY 1994 WHEN DRAMATIC events began to take place. I had been praying for over 1½ years about the decision to quit my job and get into full-time ministry. There was uncertainty everywhere I turned. It seemed to me that there were too many things to handle. After enjoying a quiet and peaceful life in India, here everything seemed to have an element of uncertainty.

Devika, the maid who worked in our home, told Angie that I was soon going to leave the country. I asked her how she knew that. She told me that while she was praying, Jesus appeared to her and told her that I would soon leave the country. I could not believe my ears. I did not even possess a passport at that time. However, I kept these things in my heart. It was at this time that I met Onasis. He was a friend of Steve, my younger brother. Onasis told me that he had seen me in a dream. I was seen wearing a blue shirt, carrying some baggage and about to leave the country. I simply could not believe these things. I prayed concerning all of it.

The Lord began to show me Singapore in my dreams. Night after night I saw different places. I saw the clean streets and the high-rise buildings. Since I had never been out of the country, I did not know what to make of it. Meanwhile, Pastor Martin called me to the front of the church to be dedicated for ministry, along with Mohan, another friend, during the Sunday morning worship service. The people of the church sent us away with their prayers and blessings. As I came out, I met a man who walked up to me. He said, "Sundar, I know that you are not the type who pushes your way around. I heard you are going to Singapore. If you do not ask people unashamedly outside this country, you will get nothing. So be bold and tell people your need. Only then can you survive. Anyway, this is my advice for you, All the best."

He turned around and walked away, while I stood there stunned. Alone under the trees, just outside the church, I prayed to God. "Lord, if you have indeed called me to be your servant, this is the covenant I make with you. I will trust you, no matter what. I know that no one who trusts in you will be disappointed. I know the righteous are never forsaken. You are my Heavenly Father and *Jehovah Jireh*, my Provider. Even if I have to suffer lack and maybe die in the process of following you, I am ready. I will not let anyone know my needs. I will only speak to you about them. It is from you that I will receive what I need." But for now, my biggest problem was the money I needed. Since I did not have sufficient finances to handle my needs, I prayed fervently.

The Lord took me to a passage in 1 Kings 17:4. *"You will drink from the brook, and I have ordered the ravens to feed you there."* Elijah was in great need. How could a prophet who walked in close relationship with God ever run into such extreme situations? I concluded that it must be a temporary phase and not a permanent condition of life. God cannot forsake his servants. It was not a financial trouble, just a spiritual test to prepare him for a supernatural provision. Strangely, I knew that the only option ahead for me was to borrow! I had lived a very content life till that point in time. I was aware that God had promised to bless me, as I was His son. He had given me the promise that I would not borrow but rather lend. I knew God as *Jehovah Jireh*, the One who supplies all my needs. However, the reality of my situation brought me to this point. I was about to borrow!

I realized I needed to do whatever God told me to do, even if at that time it defied all the logic of my brain cells. I must be willing to be led by the Spirit of God. The Lord prompted me to borrow specifically from my good friend, Mahboob Khan. After struggling in prayer, I asked Mahboob if I could see him at the office. I trembled with fear. This was the first time I had ever approached anyone for a financial favor. When I explained to Mahboob, he was only delighted to help. Within minutes the money was on his table. He told me that it was unusual for him not to change the unused foreign currency he had left after returning from an overseas trip. "I do not know why I have been holding on to these seventeen Singaporean dollars. Perhaps you will need it when you take a cab from the airport to the city." I was surprised. I was not even sure that I would be able to get the visa to go overseas but here I was being provided with the taxi fare. I felt that God was making the impossible possible. I promised Mahboob that I would return the money just before I left the country. I purchased the air ticket and applied for the visitors' visa. My cousin's wife, Grace, told me to procure a return ticket so that it would be easy for me to get the tourist visa. Even though I would not need the return ticket, I agreed to purchase it since it cost me only a marginal amount.

Things became difficult for me at the bank. They were in no mood to help me in settling my dues. I made several appeals but did not find a solution. I knew I had upset them. When I submitted my resignation, I decided to be honest concerning the reason for my resignation. So I wrote a short testimony in the resignation letter. "God has been merciful and saved a wretched sinner like me. It is not right for me to selfishly work at the bank when so many have never heard about Jesus, who alone can save people from their sin. Since I am convinced that I need to share my faith with others, I find it impossible to continue at the bank. I am grateful for the opportunity to work all these years." As my superiors read my resignation they advised me to write a simple letter.

I told them that I needed to give a legitimate reason and that was it! It simply delayed the settlement. As the day approached, I knew I could not keep the promise. Two days before I needed to leave, I found myself in an embarrassing situation. How would I face Mahboob Khan? I prayed that the Lord would make a way. That very morning, Mahboob called me on the phone. He told me that he wanted to see Angie and me that evening. So along with his wife, he came over and picked us up. I did not know what to say. He drove us right into a posh hotel. He silenced my protest by saying he wanted a quiet place with us both. I was in no mood to relish a buffet. He got my plate filled and then broke the silence. He said, "Last night the Lord told me not to take back the money from you. I told the Lord I was only too glad to help such a special friend." Early the next morning, as he was brushing his teeth, his wife Aruna, walked in. She told him that she felt that they should not take back the money from Sundar! That settled it. In order to tell us of their decision, they had taken us out for dinner. Angie and I were overwhelmed with gratitude and thanks to God. He was taking us on a special journey, outside the boat!!

The news spread throughout our family about the decision I had made to quit my job. Angie was getting ready to go to her parents' home until the time of her delivery. By this time I had both the ticket and the visa to travel. My parents arranged a prayer meeting at our home. All the members of our extended family came over to our place. We had a time of worship as they placed their hands over my head, prayed and dedicated me for the ministry. It was a special moment in my life.

I shared the miraculous provision of God with my friend, Mohan, as we traveled on that flight to Singapore. When we landed, I suddenly realized that I had stepped into a new world. My only comfort was when I met with Rev. Prabhu Dass Roberts and his wife, Clara, who eventually became my family in Singapore. Life in Singapore was like turning on the lights in a dark place. Everything was different from my life in India. First, the money I had at hand seemed to instantaneously shrink. Within the first week, I felt like a pauper in a prosperous nation. I feared the worst. The college authorities wondered how I could study there without a scholarship and without sufficient finances. Others wanted to know why I chose Singapore since it was affordable to study back in India. The immigration authorities wanted to know the justification for extension of a tourist visa. Time was running out and so were the meager resources I had with me. I wished I could leave the country secretly. I felt like Jonah.

The lady at the desk asked, "How do you think God can help you when you have not even applied for a scholarship?" I replied, "I believe that God will perform a miracle." When the immigration officer extended my visa for the last time I told him, "I know God will perform a miracle." He said, "Are you out of your mind?" I returned home disappointed and spent the night in prayer.

It was in a time like this that God gave me the song, *A Mustard Seed of Faith*. I realized that the silence of God was not the absence of God. I needed to experience Him. He had promised never to leave me or forsake me. I knew He was with me, but I felt I was groping in the dark. I sang the song by faith as if all my mountains had faded away. I had poured out my heart to God and yet nothing seemed to happen. I felt like quitting. Did I really hear from the Lord? Did I not rely on his promises? Did He not provide for me to get here? Did He not show me this place in my dreams? Did He not speak to me clearly from His word? The answers were a resounding "Yes!"

My present experience was quite the opposite. Now I could not take it any longer. I told my fellow students that I was planning to return. I shared this with the friends I had made in church. I talked to my teachers and the Dean of Students at the college. It was farewell time. I had come to the end of the road. I said, "Lord, I am about to do the wrong thing. I am not able to hang on here anymore. Please forgive me Lord." By this time I had lost between 18 to 20 pounds in weight because I could not afford to eat.

It did not take long to pack my suitcase since I had just a few things. I called Angie. She prayed and encouraged me to hang in there. I prayed for the last time before making the final decision. "Lord, I am asking you for the last time. If you do not do something for me now, I will be forced to leave. Please help me. Perform a miracle for me." As I always did, I opened the Bible to read. In Mark 7:31-37 I read the account of how Jesus healed a man who was deaf and dumb. He said, *"Be opened!"* I read how people were overwhelmed with amazement. *"He has done everything well."* As I read this passage, I felt this is what people are going to say concerning me when Jesus performs miracles in my life. He will do everything for me. Everything! I was convinced and with great peace in my heart, I removed the contents of my baggage and rearranged my belongings on the shelf. All I needed to do was to wait for the miracle to take place.

That Sunday I went back to church to attend the worship service. At the end of it, Mr. Gunaseelan, a prominent lay leader walked up to me and said, "I have been watching you for a couple of weeks here. Are you new to this place?" I rattled off my story. I told him my journey and my experiences with God. He said that Singapore was an expensive place and that students from Singapore even go to India to study over there. I told him that God had specifically sent me over here. He asked me if I had a scholarship to study. I told him that I did not have one and that I was trusting God for a miracle.

Then he told me that he wanted me to listen to his story. "Although my parents hail from Sri Lanka, I was born in Malaysia. So I am Sri Lankan by race and Malaysian by citizenship. While attending Sunday worship service when I was 17 years old, my pastor became ill during the service. With no one to help, I volunteered to go up to the front and share the word of God. The congregation was so appreciative of my contribution that they encouraged me to go to Bible College and return to pastor the same church. I was convinced that I should become a pastor. However, my life took another turn. I married early and had an opportunity to study in the United Kingdom. I completed a three-year program in 1½ years. I was offered a good job in Singapore and eventually settled here as a citizen. I have had this question in my heart? 'Why has God blessed me? Why have I not become the pastor people said I would become someday?' I have found no answers. Today I think I know why! God has blessed me in order that I could bless you so that you could become that pastor that I could really never become!"

I was shell-shocked. He then asked me what it cost to study at Trinity Theological College. I told him I had covenanted with God not to tell anyone my needs. He said he would find out. He asked me if I could come to the church the following day. When I arrive at church, he was ready and waiting for me. He had gone to the college to get the information he needed. On a printed sheet I saw he had done all the calculations. It accommodated every item of expenditure for a student for six months. It also had provision for my wife and two children. Angie and David were in India and Esther was yet to be born! I feared to see the amount at the bottom. It was a staggering 9,800 Singaporean dollars! He gave me a copy and the other one he tucked into his pocket. "Sundar," he said, "from now on you should not be worried about money. Study and equip yourself to become a pastor." Stunned and with tears running down my cheeks I returned to my apartment. The ravens brought what I needed. I had never met this man before, but God provided for me! I knew, no matter what, the Lord is faithful to all His promises.

I can never forget Mr. Gunaseelan. Later on he helped me get a scholarship that covered my studies for three years. He and his wife, Eunice, became our family. With their love and support, God helped us throughout the next three years of my student life. My financial status ever since is simply Eph. 3:20!

Ten years later the Gunaseelans were visiting India. While I was preaching at a wedding service, I saw them in the congregation. At the end of the service, he came and hugged me and said, "Sundar, it was worth the investment." How I praised God!

The Surprise Visit Home

IT WAS SEPTEMBER 1994 AND I HAD ALREADY SPENT two months in Singapore. More than being a student at the Trinity Theological College, I spent every night in prayer. I could hardly sleep. I did not fit into the study program. My health was failing and without much money in hand, I hardly ate. I lost around twenty pounds in weight.

Then the Lord miraculously provided for me through Mr. Gunaseelan. I could hardly believe the miracle. I now had my admission to school confirmed and the student visa to go with it. I had reconciled to the fact that I could not go home until I graduated, for the next three years. I knew God wanted me to learn some precious lessons in the College as well as in my personal life.

It was at this time that I met Jeeva. He had come to Singapore and through the many struggles he faced he came to put his faith in Jesus. We became friends. He wanted to know what God was teaching me on a daily basis. I had to have something to tell him each evening. Every day we met and fellowshipped together. I cherished those days. However, my struggles and the tearful conversations with Angie seemed to subside a bit by this time. Now I had to catch up for the days and weeks I had lost due to the various problems I had faced. Back in India, Angie was expecting our second child, Esther. Walking down the road with a friend one evening, I seemed to stop half way. I felt in my heart that Angie was developing labor pains. The following Sunday morning I went to church. At the end of the worship service, I stood in line along with others to shake hands with Pastor Prabhu Dass Roberts.

He looked at me and said, "Congratulations! Your wife, Angie, has delivered a baby girl! Your dad called me up just before the service commenced to convey the good news. He could not speak to you since you do not have a personal number to call." I was overjoyed on hearing the news. I was also very sad. I thought to myself, *I must be the one to tell everyone of the good news.* I said, "Lord, if you want me to go through this feeling, then may it be so." Meanwhile, Mr. Gunaseelan who was standing nearby came over to congratulate me. He asked me as to when I had planned to fly home to be with my wife and see the newborn baby. I told him that I wasn't planning to do so since an air ticket was not something I could afford as a student. I also told him that Angie and I had talked about it earlier and that she did not expect to see me in India for the next three years. He said, "I am sure Angie must be expecting you. I think you should go and visit her and see the baby."

I wished he would not continue the conversation because I was really longing to be home for a short visit. I told him that we should change the topic and he told me that if I would ask him to, he would be willing to get me an air ticket for the trip. He said if I was interested I should call his number by 10:00 that night. I returned from the church with tears and with great excitement. Would I be able to go home? Is this all true? I eagerly waited for the clock to strike 10:00! It seemed to be the longest day of my life! In my heart I knew I could not ask anyone a favor. It was with mixed feelings that I approached the public telephone booth. As I dialed the number, Mr. Gunaseelan was waiting on the other line. Before I could find the words, he said, "Sundar, thanks for calling. I know how you feel. You do not have to say a word. I want you to come to the church office by 10:00 in the morning. I will work out your ticket by that time."

I barely slept that night. Is it really going to take place? Am I going to see my wife and my family? My heart was pounding all through the night. I prayed a lot and went to bed. The next morning I got up with anticipation and went to the church office as instructed. The church secretary conveyed a message from Mr. Gunaseelan. He was sorry. There were no flights available for India during the week. My hopes came crashing down. I held back my tears. Thoroughly disappointed, I cried all the way back to my apartment. "Lord, I never even desired it in the first place. Why this offer and why this disappointment? What do you really want from me?"

When I reached the apartment, it struck me that I had booked a return ticket myself while applying for a visitor's visa to get to Singapore. I rummaged through the things on my shelf and found the ticket. I realized that it had a three-month validity period. With fresh hope, I ran back to the church office. The secretary told me to take it to the ticketing office and check to see if they had a confirmed seat for me to fly to India. In a flash I darted out to locate the Air India office. Finding my way there for the very first time was quite an ordeal. I entered the office with a prayer. There were hardly any people at the office. The lady at the desk asked if she could help me. I showed her my ticket and asked her if it was still valid. When she responded positively, I asked her if I could travel to India.

"Sir, when do you want to travel?" she asked. I told her I would like to travel at the earliest date possible. She said there was a seat on a flight that very evening. I looked stunned. I knew in my mind it was an impossible situation. Yet the seat was available. She saw the stunned look on my face and wanted to know if I was all right. I could not explain the feeling. Within the next few minutes, I had the airport tax paid and a confirmed ticket to fly to India. "Sir, you have a confirmed ticket on the 9:30 p.m. flight. Be at the airport no later than 7:30 and have a great trip." All of this took just five minutes. Here I was, standing outside with a confirmed ticket in my hands. Tears flowed down my cheeks. God must have worked out a grand plan to the minutest details!

I ran back to the church office all excited. I was asked to wait for Mr. Gunaseelan. As he pulled into the parking lot, I went out to meet him. He told me that I must not waste my time talking and must get ready to leave. "I am happy for you. Have a safe trip. Get something for your wife and baby. Good wishes to them from me. Get yourself a ticket from India when you return since it would be cheaper than getting it here." Then he tucked something into my pocket and was gone in a flash. As he left, I realized I was holding a thousand dollar bill!

Why did he do this? His love, affection and generosity reminded me of the great love of God. We don't receive his love because we deserve it. God loves us simply because HE loves us. It is impossible to find a reason why God loves us. That's the beauty of His love. Thank you Jesus!

As I settled down at my window seat, a lady wanted me to exchange it with her. Seeing how readily I gave it up, she entered into a conversation with me. I told her that I was going home to see my wife and our newborn baby. She asked me when I had booked the ticket. I told her my story. She could not believe it. She said she was flying that very day because that was the only ticket available. All flights were full for six days on either side of the date of travel. I told her that nothing was impossible for God. She spontaneously responded by saying, "God is with you, young man. He will use you mightily in the coming days."

I don't think I have enjoyed a trip home like the one I had that night. What a surprise home visit it turned out to be!

The Bills Are Settled

IT WAS 1994. BY THIS TIME I HAD BEEN IN SINGAPORE as a student for two months. The events that were taking place in my life were beyond my control. I was far away from my family in India. I was trying to find out if I was in the right place. Doubts flooded my mind.

In my heart I knew I had made my decisions based on God's word and the guidance of his Spirit. My wife Angie was about to give birth to a baby. I was wondering who would pay the bills when she was admitted to the hospital. Since she was staying with her parents the last two months, Angie's parents were insisting that they would pay. My parents, on the other hand, were insisting that they would do it, since they wanted to show their support in my decision to leave my job in India and become a student in Singapore.

Away from the family and without money, I was caught up in a dilemma. I did not know what to do so I began to pray. "Lord, you promised me that you are *'able to do exceeding abundantly above all that we ask or think.'* You are my heavenly Father. I trust you more than anyone else. I do not want my father or my father-in-law to make the payments at the hospital. Since you are my heavenly Father, I want you to pay since I have obeyed you and am trusting in you."

To make a long story short, I was able to get a ticket and along with the generosity of Mr. Gunaseelan and God's provision I arrived in India. That was a night of surprises for my family. I waited until I arrived in India to let them know of my visit. My parents were overjoyed. I did not get to my father-in-law's residence (where Angie was staying) until 2.00 a.m. When I knocked on the door, it was my mother-in-law who came to the door and opened it. It was an open and shut experience. She thought she had seen a ghost! I believe this was the only time I managed to scare my mother-in-law! Meanwhile, David woke up and hid in excitement. He could not believe that his dad had come to be with him. It was a memorable experience.

I talked to Angie about the experience she had in the hospital. I was curious to know who finally ended up paying the bills. "How much did your father pay? We have to settle the bills with him." She told me her father did not pay anything. I thought perhaps my father had paid but Angie told me that he did not pay either. "Then who did pay?" I asked with much curiosity. Angie told me this story.

On the day she had delivered Esther, her friend and colleague, Anna, was leaving the university to head to the hospital to capture the first picture of Esther on her camera. As Anna was leaving, she met a friend of hers who wanted to tag along and see the newborn baby. When this friend met Angie, she was curious to know why Angie's husband was missing. She was told the story about how I had resigned my job, sold everything and gone to Singapore for training to serve the Lord. She could not believe the story! Later that day Anna and her friend left the hospital. Two days later, Angie was about to be discharged. Her dad, after convincing my parents that he would make the payments, went to settle the bills. When he arrived at the desk he was told that the bills had already been settled! He could not believe it. When he questioned the hospital staff, they told him that a lady settled it two days ago! This lady had asked them when Angie would be discharged and how much the final bill would be. Then she pulled out her checkbook and wrote the exact amount in final settlement of Angie's bill. She requested that they not mention this to anyone.

Praise the Lord! God had heard my prayers. It was my heavenly Father who settled my bills!

Part III
Pain to Pupose

From left to right: Sundar, his mother Dulcie Moses, in front of her Sundar's younger brother, Stephen, sister Suganthi Asokan, his father Dhanapal Moses and his father's sister Jessie Moses

The Moses cricket team of cousins! Sundar Moses second from right

Sundar, his parents and his brother

Sundar Moses with his friends at his engagement ceremony

Sundar and Angie with Sundar"s spiritual mother, Annie Johnson, at their engagement ceremony

A packed church at the wedding ceremony in Chennai January 4, 1990,

Mr. and Mrs. Moses on their wedding day

James Santhosham, a former Hindu priest who met Jesus, praying for the couple at the wedding

Angie and Sundarsingh Moses as newly married

Sundar Moses (second from left) with Mahboob Khan and other friends

Esther gets a ride from Dad

Mrs. Purnima Revis, former President of Isabella Thoburn College, shows Sundar Moses Sadhu Sundar Singh"s eating plate

The extended Moses family on the beach outside Chennai

Trinity Theological College M. Div Class

Mr. and Mrs. Moses Sr, in Chennai

The Moses family at a wedding.

From left: David, Esther, Lydia, Angie and Sundar

Lal Bagh Methodist Church in Lucknow

Rev. Moses dedicating thirteen babies, who were born after a very special prayer

Young lady (to the left) healed from cancer

The lady for whom God "tampered with the 'solar' system"

A GLOMOS student in Sri Lanka healed from arthritis

A lady, who was healed from cancer, greeted after church service by Rev. and Mrs. Moses

Sundarsingh and Angie Moses in their home in Lucknow

Lars Dunberg and Sundar Moses deliberate the future at a leadership meeting in India

"You are like Moses– step out in faith!" Lennart Hambre from the Global Action Board with Sundar and Angie Moses in Lucknow October 2006

*Lecturing at GLOMOS in San Pedro Sula,
Honduras 2009*

*"Now, this is what you do!"
Counseling a young man at a
Youth gathering in Hyderabad
October 2009*

*"Don"t despair, God will help you
through this!" Giving advice at the
New Generation conference in
Orissa 2007*

*I said, "I want to see Jesus!
That is my heart"s desire!"*

Teaching 2,200 people at the New Generation Youth Convocation in Bhubaneswar, Orissa October 2007

Lars Dunberg, Sundarsingh Moses and Supratim Dey of Action Ministries in traditional garb in Kalimpong

Outstanding GLOMOS graduate gets his special award from the hands of Sundarsingh Moses, July 2010

GLOMOS graduate receives his certificate in Lucknow July 2010

Rev. Moses speaking at a Men's conference in Kalimpong October 2008

Rev. Sundar Moses sharing his heart with a leader in the Himalayas

A GLOMOS graduate pastor in Lucknow (right) whose congregation grew three times in one year

Young man whose broken back was healed. Here with his family

Rev. Sundar Moses addressing the graduates in Lucknow July 2010, interpreted by Dr. Usha Solomon, herself a GLOMOS teacher

The Dead Are Raised!

IT WAS 1996. WE WERE GETTING CLOSE TO THE CHRIST-mas season and we had the privilege to come home to India as a family for the first time while I was a student in Singapore. It was not only time to celebrate Christmas with our family but also to celebrate two family weddings.

During the last week in December my brother Steve was getting married. During the first week of January Pearline, Angie's sister was getting married. As is the Indian custom, Angie and I personally carried wedding invitation cards with us and visited several homes. It was a time to reconnect with friends and family members we had not seen for a couple of years, since moving to Singapore. It was also a time to share our experiences with them and share what God was doing in our lives. Angie and I hired a car and traveled to every nook and cranny of the city with the invitations.

Every day we tried to catch up with the long list. In India the wedding is more a community event than a family affair. While we scheduled a day's activity together, almost every day we returned not having covered the list for the day. It was quite tiring even though we were excited to meet people. Several times, I felt a strain in my heart leading to discomfort. I attributed it to the extra effort we were putting in.

One night as we traveled on one of the visits, the car broke down in the middle of an overpass, causing a huge traffic jam. Meanwhile a policeman on duty came over and yelled at us to get the vehicle out of the way. He himself lent a helping hand. Others joined in the act. After several attempts to try and get the car moving had proved futile, I decided to give it one more attempt. It was then that I felt an excruciating pain in my heart. As we moved to a poorly lit place, I asked a passerby to help one more time. Together we tried again with the man at the wheel and Angie seated inside. We failed this time too. While those who helped moved on, I realized the pain in my heart was becoming unbearable. It was like having a spear run through my heart. I knew I was going to collapse. I was looking for a place to sit and rest a while. I knew if I did not do something soon, I would collapse on the sidewalk.

Seeing a little gate leading to a pathway in front of a set of apartments, I managed to open the gate and get in. I had barely made it in when I realized I was passing out. I rushed ahead. As I neared the flight of stairs, I collapsed. I tried to call for help but I realized that I did not have an ounce of strength left in me. Then I began to lose all my faculties. I felt like everything around me was becoming dark as my eyes were beginning to shut. I tried to scream at the top of my voice but no sound was produced. I tried to motion with my hands but I couldn't make any gestures. I couldn't move my fingers. As I lay there, one by one my body functions began to cease. First, I lost my ability to move. Then I realized I had lost my speech and hearing. Finally my vision was gone and I lost control of my bladder. I began to perspire profusely. Then something strange began to take place. I began to lose sensation in my toes and it seemed to move on to my upper body. I could not feel my ankles, then my knees, thighs or hips. I knew I was going to die. I felt as if life itself was going out of my body. I had never experienced anything like this before. I do not remember what took place after that. I was completely incoherent.

While the light had faded, Angie, unaware of what had taken place, got out of the car to search for me. She could not find me anywhere. She asked somebody, "Did you see a man pushing this car?" They did not know whom she was referring to. She hurried up and down the street making further enquiries but to no avail. Now she began to panic. She desperately pleaded with people passing by for help. In fear, she began to call out my name aloud. There was no response. I do not know how long it took her but about 15 minutes later, she saw a gate that was left open. She rushed in to see if possibly I was there. As she entered she saw my feet at the beginning of the flight of stairs. She could not see my body though. Agitated and angry for lack of any response to her call, she came in and yelled at me. "Why are you lying down here? Did you not hear me call you all this time? Why did you not respond? Why are you so silent?"

By this time she realized that my body was lifeless. She realized I was not just resting; I was gone! She began to cry uncontrollably. She then raised her voice to God in prayer. "Jesus! Jesus! Save my husband! Jesus! Save my husband!" While she prayed and cried, life gradually came back into my body. I began to regain consciousness. The whole process that I had gone through seemed to revert. I regained my faculties all over again. I went from having blurred vision to feeling that everything had cleared up. Then I saw the face of Angie so close to mine. I could see the anxiety on her face. With mixed emotions, she asked me if I was all right. I told her I was. By this time, my body had become hard as wood and cold as ice. Meanwhile, the friend of mine at the wheel, returned after a futile search for me in another direction. In a flash he lifted my body, put me in the rear seat of the car and drove me home. I really did not comprehend what had happened. We were too shocked and stunned to share it with anyone.

I spent the night in silence trying to relive the experience of being brought back to life. That day I knew how powerful the name of Jesus is. I was glad that God had given me a wife who would not give up. What a great miracle! I realized that the Bible is true. Hebrews 11:35, *"Women received back their dead, raised to life again."* What a great Jesus! What an awesome Name. The Name that is above all Names, Jesus.

How Great Is His Joy In the Victory That He Gives!

I WAS INVITED TO SPEAK AT A RETREAT IN ANOTHER city on August 15, 2001. While I was returning home to Lucknow, I found out that Angie had fainted while attending her college program and had to be hospitalized. I did not know that the incident would have a long-term consequence for her.

On visiting her at the hospital, I was asked by the doctors to get a particular medication that could control her blood pressure. I was on the road for the next three days hoping to get the prescribed medicines. After the search, the supplier told me that the medication was not available in the city. Meanwhile, my parents and friends back in Chennai were concerned that Angie had been hospitalized for four days already.

Mahboob Khan called me and said, "Sundar, if Angie requires better treatment I can send you a ticket to fly her back to Chennai. Just send her over here and we will take care of her." I replied, "Mahboob, I am really tempted to accept your kind offer but we have come here trusting God. It is here we need to experience His hand of grace over our lives." Since I would not send Angie to him, Mahboob managed to get the medicines imported and sent them to me. These medicines were categorized as a "life-saving drug" so the pilot of a local airline decided to get the drugs to me as quickly as possible and sent them directly to my home through his friend. I was encouraged by these gestures and concluded that God was really with us.

I was expecting Angie to recover quickly. On rushing to the hospital with the medicine, I was asked to meet a doctor who wanted me to sign some documents. I was surprised that they were not interested in looking at the medication they had requested. Instead they advised me to get her to another hospital. Naively I asked them when I could bring her back. They told me I did not need to bring her back to the hospital again. Then

I realized they had discharged her! In fact they dismissed her from the hospital. I was agitated. Some friends from the church wanted me to give them a piece of my mind. In my heart I knew that God had other plans for Angie.

I quickly took her to the state-run hospital even though I knew the facilities were poor in comparison to the one she had been in. As I went up the stairs, I felt a strange peace that flooded my heart. I immediately told Angie that it was here that she would recover from her illness. We met a nurse, the wife of a friend of mine, at the hospital. She wanted to help us since she worked there. After looking at Angie's file, she told me that only God had saved her life. She told me, "Do not be upset that they did not treat your wife well at the previous hospital. God Himself got her out of there. If they would have continued the dosage they had been administering, your wife would be dead by now." I thanked God.

The first couple of days were quite horrible to say the least. During the day, I watched rats run all over the place. For almost every patient admitted, there were more than two from the family looking after him or her. The ward had over 25 beds lined up. I saw people everywhere. It was unhygienic. I also came to know they had power shortages. I rushed back to borrow a battery-operated fan that could run for four hours a day. As I returned home late in the night the scene was always the same: driving back with tears and prayers. Within a few days at the hospital, Angie contracted a urinary infection as well.

Then we were offered a special private room. I was told it was available because no one else would take it. Someone had died from AIDS the previous day in that private room. After the fumigation I went in and prayed and then we were ready to move Angie in. The doctors told me that she needed to stay in the hospital until her blood pressure could be controlled. She would need to be there for at least a month.

Meanwhile, the church was getting ready for a worship concert that involved four churches from four different denominations. The choir members wanted me to postpone the event. I told them, "It is at a time like this that we should exercise our faith in God." Although it was difficult to go through practice sessions for the concert, take care of the two children, attend to pastoral responsibilities and preach the sermons, I knew God was in control. The choir members went to the hospital the night before the concert to sing and cheer Angie up. We cherished the gesture.

I could feel the Lord urging me to go into a period of fasting to seek His will regarding Angie's sickness. As I continued to fast and pray while attending to all the pastoral work, I experienced much fatigue. I had never disclosed my own sickness to anyone. The devil seemed to wear me down. I had so many questions and concerns. He seemed to say, "How long will you continue the fast? You will affect your own health. Soon both of you will be sick. Who will take care of your family? What will happen to your ministry?" I felt so discouraged. God enabled me to persevere. On the seventh day of the fast I read Psalm 21. *"O Lord, the king rejoices in your strength. How great is his joy in the victories you give! You have granted him the desire of his heart and have not withheld the request of his lips."*

As I meditated on these words, I felt a great joy flood my heart. How could I possibly be happy while my wife was in the hospital? Lord, Are you telling me something I need to know? Then I understood. The Lord was telling me that Angie was all right even before the doctors could tell me. I jumped with joy. I quickly prepared some breakfast and rushed to the hospital. As usual, Angie was concerned about me. "Are you fasting today as well?" she asked. I replied, "Today I am about to break the fast since the Lord has healed you."

So, I shared the excitement of what God had done in my heart. I told her that God put an emotion in my heart much before the event took place. We thanked the Lord and enjoyed breakfast together at the hospital. In the morning the doctor came on her regular visit and said, "Angie, suddenly things are looking better for you. I think in all probability, you can be discharged tomorrow!" We shed tears and thanked the Lord.

Soon Angie was back and God saw her through the pregnancy. Lydia was born on October 20, 2001.

The Long and Dark Tunnel

SEEING ME AGAIN AFTER A FEW YEARS, SOMEONE asked this question, "Sundar! Something about you has changed! What happened to your moustache?" With a smile on my face I said, "Did you not know that a few years ago I had a close shave?"

It was the year 2004. I was in my eighth year of seeking to understand God's purpose for the pain I was experiencing.

As I wrote in a previous section of this book, during my student days in Singapore my family and I had the opportunity to visit India and participate in two weddings. One wedding was Angie's sister, Pearline, and the other was my brother, Steve's. In India, the wedding custom is to deliver the invitations in person. With two weddings and almost all of my extended family in Chennai, I knew it would be nothing less than a miracle to get the cards to everyone on our planned list. As we rushed to deliver the invitations, I went into massive cardiac arrest and was clinically dead for at least fifteen minutes.

When Angie found my motionless body—knowing that only God could save me—in faith she cried out loud, "Jesus! Help my husband!" In the 11th chapter of Hebrews the writer describes faith as the *"assurance of things hoped for, the conviction of things not seen."* Angie had an assurance that God would hear her prayer and help her husband, exactly what she hoped for. Therefore, she experienced what we read in Hebrews 11:35, *"Women received back their dead, raised to life again. Praise God!"*

I was taken to a hospital and only 40 seconds into a treadmill test the doctors concluded that I suffered from serious heart disease. While the doctor was advising me on the steps I needed to take, I heard an audible voice saying, *My son, they will bring you to a hospital another time. They will give you a checkup and declare you fit!*

I was stunned at the voice and decided that I would pray before seeking any additional medical help. After three days of fasting and prayer, Sister Rani Roberts declared that the hand of the Lord was on my heart and that I should return to Singapore. Miraculously I was able to purchase an air ticket that would take me back to Singapore just a few days later to complete my final semester of the M. Div. program.

Upon my return, life was hard. I had only enough strength to take about five steps at a time. After that effort I would have to stop and rest in order to catch my breath. I claimed the power in the blood of Christ for every step I took. Fortunately, my condition improved daily as I felt a remarkable strength in my body. I was able to carry my young children on my shoulders, participate in sports activities and lift heavy things as well. In a few months I graduated with the best grades of the final semester. Now we were ready to return to India!

I was appointed Pastor of the Thoburn Memorial Methodist Church in Kolkata, India. As I prepared to take up the responsibility of leading a church, I received a call from the bishop informing me that plans had been altered. I was reappointed as the Pastor of the Lal Bagh Methodist Church in Lucknow.

When we arrived in Kolkata, someone had broken into our container and we lost many things. Stunned with this loss, the Lord spoke to me saying, *My son, remember when you arrived in Singapore with a single bag, I promised you that I would bless you like Jacob when you return to India. Do not worry that you have lost these things. I have another opportunity to bless you all over again!* Ready to break into tears of disappointment over our loss, I told Angie what the Lord had said to me. It was a great experience. I shared it with the officials at the port. They were amazed at my response to the situation. It gave me a great opportunity to share my faith in Jesus with them. I then got our remaining belongings repacked and traveled for over 24 hours to our new home, Lucknow.

As you might expect, the first few days in Lucknow were extremely stressful. Aside from the stress of travel to a new ministry and home, lawlessness, kidnapping, shooting, corruption and injustice were freely practiced in the society to levels I had never known. Too scared to read the newspaper, I discontinued the habit for a while. I pondered over these things through many a restless night. I wished I could change the plans God had for me! I realized that only when you sincerely want to do God's will are you tested to the limit. Once again I shed tears and spent a lot of time in prayer. To further our struggle, this new church situation was not good either. There were only 12 people present at my first worship service as Pastor of this historic church.

From the very first day of serving the Lord in Lal Bagh Methodist Church I disqualified myself because of my health issues. I reminded the Lord that a person called to serve must have at least some minimum level of health. The Lord chose to encourage me in my discouragement. I was asked if I could host a Pastors' Seminar for the Methodist Church in our region. I happily obliged knowing this was an opportunity to encourage those involved in ministry in this region.

As I sat through the sessions, I could not understand anything that was said because it was conducted in the local language. Sitting at the rear of the auditorium and with nothing to keep my attention, I began to question God about my health and my ministry. As is my way when searching for answers, I flipped through the pages of my Bible and the Lord began to speak to me from a passage in Isaiah.

I read the account of King Hezekiah's sickness and testimony. I knew I needed to wait for the Lord's time in my life. My eyes stopped on Isaiah 38:15-16. *"But what can I say? He has spoken to me, and he himself has done this. I will walk humbly all my years because of this anguish of my soul. Lord, by such things men live; and my spirit finds life in them too. You restored me to health and let me live."*

How I wished I could write the account of God restoring me to health someday! I still did not understand completely but accepted my heart condition as a loving and purposeful act of God. I ran home to share this with Angie. I was convinced that the day would come when God would restore me to health again.

Since I could not enjoy a simple meal or recline in order to sleep at night, I decided I would put my time to good use. The Lord allowed me to enjoy spending nights in prayer. Being new to the community—I hardly knew people in this city—allowed me the privilege of long seasons of prayer. Being fearful, I prayed that God would assist me as I handled the challenges in ministry. These factors contributed to my prayer life. It was not unusual for me to spend up to sixteen hours in prayer daily during that phase of my ministry. During this time the Lord brought what seemed to be impossible situations before me. God performed miraculous miracles as I came alongside people, prayed and wept with them. Now I had stories and experiences of people that were etched in my memory by the hand of God.

With no sign of any relief in my health, I was often so exhausted physically that I was tempted to lie on a bed while making pastoral visits in hospitals. Many times I felt their problems were small when compared to mine. Not surprisingly, as the miracles multiplied I began to wonder why the Lord—who performed miracles when I interceded for others—would not be gracious and turn in my direction for a change. This question continued to plague me for the next eight years. I held on to the Lord and remembered the words He had spoken to me in the hospital—*My son, they will bring you to a hospital another time. They will give you a check-up and declare you fit!* I knew nothing would ever change that truth. I would not deny the experience even though doubts assailed me.

In 2002 I had the opportunity to teach in the Global Module Studies Program (GLOMOS), a pastoral training program of *Global Action* in New Delhi. In the middle of the night on the second night there, I woke up struggling to breathe. The thought flashed through my mind that, on the following day, the local newspaper would include an article about me: Pastor From the Methodist Church in Lucknow Found Dead in Hotel Room! Fear gripped me. I began to pray and then I heard an audible voice, "Sundar!" I jumped out of bed in pure delight. I had heard the Lord call me by name! Unable to sleep, I sat up through the night waiting to hear the other things He might have to say to me. Sadly, that never happened but I realized I was all right and back to normal. By then it was 5:30 in the morning. I decided to prepare for the teaching I had to do that day.

On the concluding day of the course, Reshmi, one of the students, insisted that I meet her husband, Ajit. Upon meeting him for the first time, Ajit said, "Brother Moses, we have not met but I know you. As believers we do not need to meet in person to get to know each other." I was surprised. He continued, "You have already had a major situation concerning your heart. Do not worry. This is the Lord's doing!" I was speech-less. This experience gave me a supernatural ability to believe in God and trust in Him, no matter what the circumstances.

As we were nearing the 2003 Christmas season, ministry responsibilities took a heavy toll on my physical condition. The congregation had now grown to over 300 people in attendance every Sunday. We began to have some good problems. Several issues had to be handled directly or indirectly in the church; seating capacity, parking problems, water supply, power prob-lems, and the renovation of the church building which was built in 1870. All of these *good problems* became *big challenges*. It seemed impossible to move ahead with these responsibilities considering my limited health. As I studied the scriptures one morning, Angie and I read about the shoot from the stump of Jessie in Isaiah 11:1-2. We concluded that there was hope be-yond our situation. We praised and worshipped the Lord for the encouragement we had received that morning and I decid-ed to get ready for another day at the office. Little did I know what I had ahead of me that day.

I was seated in the restroom when I felt my head spin. I fell to the floor and that was the last thing I remembered until I saw Angie's frightened face before me. When I fell to the floor I had hit my face against the faucet and was bleeding from my chin and lips. On hearing the thud, Angie came rushing in to see a frightening but familiar sight, the limp and lifeless body of her husband on the floor. With help that only God could possibly provide, she lifted me up and life came back to my body. To calm her fears, I told her that I was all right, not really knowing what had taken place. I stood under the shower and regained my composure. In the meantime, Angie brought me a cup of tea. I got dressed and bent down to put on my socks. There was no strength in my body to do even that.

Once again I heard the familiar voice of the Lord, *My son, you have been through much; are you willing to suffer more!* I could not believe what I had heard. When Angie arrived with the cup of tea I told her my experience. I told her that it seemed that all I had been through up and until that morning was not all there was going to be, there was more to come. The struggle was not over. I told her I wanted to take her out for a drive. She thought I was nuts! We traveled by a local tricycle. This allowed Angie to see for herself that I was back to normal. I told her I was holding onto the voice of the Lord and that He would have to speak to me specifically if I needed to go to the hospital.

In the year 2004, the Lord gave me a vision. I saw myself before the Lord. He told me that He was going to take me through a long and dark tunnel, much longer and darker than I had ever seen. I saw myself so small before Him, telling Him that I would be terrified by the experience. I saw myself asking, *"Lord, if you give me the grace to go through it, I am willing to. If you will take away my fear, then I could be a great witness for you. It is in crisis that I could be a powerful testimony. Please hear my prayer."* The Lord replied, *"I have heard your prayer. I will take away your fear but you will see people around you terrified."* When I woke up, it did not seem like a dream. It was real! I shared the vision with Angie.

One Sunday morning, I did not feel well so I delegated responsibility for the morning service to the lay people in our church. Smita Singh led in worship, Rajiv Mall led in prayer and John Khushal delivered the sermon. My life felt like it was ebbing away. Within the first 10 minutes of the worship service, I told Angie that I needed to get back to the parsonage. The members watched as I found my way back, sensing that something was wrong.

After the service, the parsonage quickly filled with people, some helping, others crying and the rest of them praying. I think I was nearing the dark tunnel God had spoken to me about. Dr. Brinda, a family friend and member of our church, wanted me to be admitted to the hospital right away. I was still waiting for God's instructions. In the morning during our quiet time, the Lord spoke through Ecclesiastes 8:5-6, *"Whoever obeys his command will come to no harm, and the wise heart will know the proper time and procedure. For there is a proper time and procedure for every matter, though a man's misery weighs heavily upon him."*

Dr. Brinda had arrived at our home early in the morning while we were discussing what we had read in our quiet time. We shared our decision with her. She was overjoyed and told us that the word *procedure*—the same word used in Ecclesiastes—was a medical term physicians would often use. Angie told me that there was nothing to worry about since the Lord had spoken to her from Psalm 18 about how the Lord had seen my situation, heard my prayers—*my cry for help before Him came into His ears*—and that He Himself would come to my aid and rescue.

The next day I checked into the hospital for an angiogram. The lady at the desk was not sure that I was the patient. I requested Veena Solomon to pray before being admitted. She prayed and committed me into the hands of the Lord even as many others joined in. There were a lot of tears. During the prayer I felt something over my hands. When I opened my eyes I saw a pair of white hands clasped around mine. Wow! I knew that the prayer of Veena was already answered. While the procedure was being performed the physicians discovered that I had almost nine arterial blockages. On the lateral descending artery alone, commonly known as the widow maker, I had as many as five arterial blocks! The doctor told me that my heart was receiving only 10% of the needed blood supply and yet had no related symptoms. When he realized how critical my situation was he became very concerned.

I knew I was approaching *the dark tunnel* the Lord had told me about earlier. With confidence I told the doctor that nothing bad would take place. He was surprised at my reassurance. I told him that I had experienced acute pain in my heart over 100 times in the past eight years. I also shared with him that God had a purpose for my life and that nothing drastic would take place until that purpose was accomplished. Ignoring me, he threw off his cap, mask and gown and fled from the room. He told Angie—waiting outside—that her husband was a ticking time bomb and that since there was no adequate facility to give immediate help, he was certain that he would lose the patient in less than 30 minutes!

It was decided that I would receive better treatment if they moved me to South India. The church decided to get tickets for the whole family and fly us to my home city, Chennai. My wife tried to call the doctor who had earlier been a member of our church in North India and who had moved there to Chennai. Angie called my sister's home to get his telephone number. My cousin who was visiting my sister at that time called the Medical Superintendent of the hospital, Dr. Roy, who happened to be my schoolmate and friend. Dr. Roy immediately called the doctor in Lucknow.

Dr. Khanna was not willing to discharge me since he felt that I could not leave the hospital in my current condition. Dr. Roy told him that he would take the responsibility for anything that happened to me. Dr. Khanna received assurance from Angie that he would not be personally responsible for anything that happened to me because I left the hospital against the doctor's advice. I was taken to the airport, flown to Delhi and eventually to Chennai in South India. An announcement was made in the aircraft that I was to be the last one to deplane. They brought a wheelchair and then I was taken into a waiting ambulance.

There were about 75 family members and friends waiting to welcome me. On reaching the hospital we had 20 minutes of worship and prayer at the entrance of the coronary care unit. Dr. Roy announced to the team of doctors that I was his friend and schoolmate. In spite of my condition the doctors declared that my heart muscle was in excellent condition. They told me that they could wait over the weekend and scheduled me for surgery on May 10, 2004. I enjoyed the quietness and privacy of the hospital ward over that weekend. I asked God to protect every person in that ward as a sign that he was with me. Many were in critical stages but over the weekend none proved fatal. Again, God answered my prayers.

It was 3.30 a.m. on the morning of Sunday May 9, 2004. I turned on the lights and was reading. The nurse walked in and asked me why I was awake. "Are you scared of the surgery? These things are normal. You will be alright." I replied that I wasn't afraid. In fact I wanted to make use of the quietness and the air conditioning to read my Bible. She told me she did not know why she had never read the Bible. I told her that it was a book about God and that when a person read His book the Author himself would speak. "Tell me what God spoke to you today?" I took out my spiritual journal and gave it to her. She read the entry for the day. Proverbs 9:11,"*For through me your days will be many, and years will be added to your life."* She was astonished. Later, she asked me if she could flip through the pages in my journal. I let her. She looked at a poem written there. "Sir, did you write this one too?" I told her God inspired my heart and I wrote it down and that it even had a tune. She asked me if I could sing it for her and I did! It was given to me as I struggled through those difficult times in life.

Thank You, Lord!

Lord I thank you for the pure joy as you came into my heart
And the great assurance that you'll never depart
In my trials and temptations, victories and defeats
The lesson that there's power as I wait just at your feet

Chorus
Thank you, O Lord (2)
How can I express the ways that I am blessed
Thank you, O Lord.

For the places that you take me to speak your Holy Word
In varied circumstances to pray in your lovely name
To experience your mighty power that saves and heals
O the pure joy that you cause me to feel

For the many special moments when I could hear you speak
And the miracles you do to supply all I need
Through dreams, thoughts and visions, promises and prophesies
Lord, I'm so amazed by the ways in which you lead

And when my strength grows weary and I can't go on anymore
When the sun refuses to shine and it's time for me to go
When my journey here is ended and I'm ready to cross this shore
To know that I will worship you in heaven for evermore

When I had finished singing the song she had tears in her eyes. She asked me if her friend could have some of my time. Before I could reply, she had run back to her apartment in the hospital to share her excitement. Soon her friend, a nurse, was at my bedside. I shared my diary, the words from the Bible and my faith in Christ. She pleaded if she could bring her friend too! Soon, I had a third nurse alongside my bed to hear my story and my journey of faith. It was about 5.30 a.m.

Even though I needed only eight bottles of blood for the surgery, about 30 persons lined up to be donors. Some of them insisted that they would want their blood to run in my body, as they were grateful for being blessed through my ministry! Another hospital donated ten bottles. The doctor asked me if I would permit them to use it for other needy patients. At the chapel over a 150 persons gathered for prayer. When anxious relatives of patients saw them, they wanted to know why so many were praying for one patient. My family and friends took this opportunity to pray and share their faith with many patients and their relatives, many came to Christ as a result. These were from South Africa, Nepal, Bangladesh, Sri Lanka and other countries. In their excitement I felt they had forgotten me! Others mobilized financial help for me to clear the medical bills that were mounting up. People I have never met before came up to contribute until all the bills were miraculously paid. Thanks be to the Lord!

After the surgery was complete, I developed complications and was placed in the intensive care unit. My blood pressure shot up to levels over 200. Further, I developed colitis and was unable to keep any medication down. My stomach suffered as well. With further medication, I also suffered with precariously low blood pressure. With the doctors trying to deal with the complications, I heard the Lord's familiar voice. *'My son, did I not tell you that the tunnel would be long and dark? This is it. I am with you.'* I was overjoyed. I told my wife when she came in about the experience. It gave me immense strength to be able to go through the ordeal.

Because of my complications, a few days after the surgery I was brought to a private room. The pain was so unbearable that I was audibly groaning. I asked if I could have some pain-killers. The nurse told me that I already had been administered the maximum dosage. I dreaded the nights because my pain became so intense. One night as I was lying in bed, sleepless due to the pain, I heard the voice of God calling me by name, *"My son, Sundar!"* The voice was different. It was incredibly loud, like a blast in my ears! I cried out in fear saying, *'Lord, do not speak to me for I will surely die.'* However, God continued to speak. I said, *'Lord, you know I am in such terrible pain. I know that if you speak one word or extend your hand to touch me, I would be instantaneously relieved of it. Why don't you help me?'* God replied, *'Did you know that there are millions of people in the world who are hurting and suffering?'*

How could I possibly claim to know that, as I am such a selfish human being, I thought to myself. I responded, "Lord, I do not know all these things." Then God said to me, *'That is why I have permitted this in your life. I want you to have a heart of compassion for them. I myself have done this! Do you know that when pain and sickness touches a person's body, they say that God does not love them? Tell them not to doubt my love for them. They will turn around and ask you, 'How do I know God loves me? If He truly does, then why am I in this terrible situation?'* He continued, *'When you are well, I will take you and make you stand before such people. Tell them that I love them. Tell them that I sent my son to die on the cross for them ready to prove my love for them. When you tell them this, I myself will reveal my glory!'*

Suddenly it occurred to me that it was God the Father speaking to me! No wonder, I was trembling in fear and crying out to Him to stop talking to me lest I die instantly. God continued to allow me to hear Him share other things in the hospital during the next few days as well! I could not share this with anybody. Who am I to hear these things? Who will believe me? Will I be creating some more controversies? Don't we have enough of them in the church already? I decided to modify my testimony! I simply told them that the Lord spoke to me while I was in the hospital.

The cardiologist, Dr. Chandrasekar, came on his usual visits. I thanked him for his help and the care given to me during the period of surgery. But, he thanked me. I asked him why. He replied, "You being here has enabled me to find God's will for my life!" I was astounded. Then he explained his situation. He told me that he had been offered a new job. It meant he was going to be paid twice as much as his present pay package but had two conditions he needed to fulfill. One, he had to give his consent and two; he had to do that within three days. The doctor told me, "Since you are my pastor and a man of God, I have to be responsible for you till you are well and discharged. So it was easy for me to say, No!" I was in tears. I felt that I was responsible for ruining his career. As this thought ran across my mind the Lord prompted me to say to him, "As a servant of the Lord, I want to let you know that this is what will happen to your life. Soon, God will open an opportunity for you much bigger than what you have given up." When I visited the hospital 18 months later, I was told he had moved on to become a partner in a hospital run by his doctor friend where he attended to all patients with heart conditions!

Of all the things that happened to me during the post-surgery period, I want to narrate just two of them related to my painful experience.

The principal of a leading institution from another city was diagnosed with cancer. Barely out of hospital and back to pastoral ministry, the Lord impressed on my heart to visit her and pray for her so we drove there as a family. When we arrived, I was told that she had been rushed to the hospital. Her relatives and family members had been informed that she had only a few hours left to live. I drove to the hospital in a hurry and was given a special privilege to meet her. As I came into the intensive care unit, I did not recognize her. She did not have even a faint resemblance of her towering personality.

As we began to sing, I heard her faint voice, "Is that you, Rev. Moses?" Looking at her, I fought back my tears. I told her, "When pain touches our body we begin to doubt the love of God. We ask Him, why do these things happen? Why me? Even if you do not understand, do not doubt the love of God. He loves you. God has already shown the extent of His love to us. He has sent His own son, Jesus, to die on the cross for us. Do you believe this?" When she smiled in response, I offered to pray. Meanwhile Angie asked me why the room was so warm. I replied that it was not due to the malfunctioning of the air conditioner, but the tangible presence of the Lord. Led by the Spirit, I rebuked the power of sickness over her life. There was many prayers and tears in that room.

When we had finished, the doctor arrived. He told us that he heard the prayers and did not want to disturb us earlier. Then he tried to cheer her up and said, "You must put on some footwear and get out of the room for a change. The fresh air will do you good." She enquired about my children. Angie replied that they were in the car outside. She desired to see them. I told her I would go and get them but she wanted to go and see them herself. So she got out of the room and walked down the corridor! I told her to wait as I could bring the children in. She said she could walk and so she stepped through the door of the hospital. I told her that I could not get a parking slot and had to park two blocks away. She insisted she could walk. As she walked with an extraordinary strength within her body, the family members were walking behind with tears in their eyes. Her husband said, "Rev. Moses, can you believe it? We all thought she would surely be gone by today. Just five minutes after the prayer she is walking down the street!" I told him, that is the power of God.

In 2008 I had the privilege to visit El Salvador for the first time, teaching in the *Global Action* pastoral and leadership training program in Central America. On the concluding day, a student took me aside and said, "Pastor Moses, I have a word from the Lord for you. The Lord tells me that you had to be hospitalized to undergo a major heart surgery. The Father himself spoke to you. God has given you a heart like that of David! Just like the Spirit came upon David from the very moment he was anointed by Samuel, God's Spirit will rest on you from now on in special and unique ways."

I was taken back, filled with joy and greatly blessed by her words. I also knew God was reminding me that I had modified my testimony to avoid a controversy. I thought to myself, "What a gentle reminder from God through this person across the globe! Surely God must be extremely sensitive and absolutely powerful! She told me that my experience is similar to the one described by the Psalmist in chapter 2 Samuel. As I read it I realized the amazing ways of God. He spoke to Angie before the surgery through Psalm 18, to me immediately after the surgery in 2004 in an audible voice and to this student across the globe through 2 Samuel 22, four years later! Could I make anything out of it? I choose to marvel at God, a vital element for a worshipping heart.

Through all of these events I learned that there is no pain without a purpose. Instead of asking, "Why the pain?" we need to ask, "For what greater purpose?" This can happen only when one is convinced that no matter what, God is a good God.

Part IV

Pastoring in a New Culture

The First Sign

IN 1997, WE ARRIVED IN THE CITY OF LUCKNOW, IN THE State of Uttar Pradesh, North India. I had just completed my three-year Master of Divinity program at the theological college in Singapore.

When I took over the responsibilities of being a pastor I faced some of the greatest challenges in my life. Uttar Pradesh is a state full of people, known for its large population. Christians account for less than half a percent of the population. My heart was burdened by this fact. I wondered if one person could make a difference.

Dwarfed by the towering church steeples and arches, overwhelmed with its history and the great pastors like Dr. E. Stanley Jones who had shepherded it in the past, I felt so small, intimidated, and inadequate. So, what did I do? I spent most of my time crying out to God in prayer. Sometimes I spent 16 hours a day in prayer. I barely slept. I walked around the church hour after hour praying, calling out to God and trying to discover what God could do.

Then I prayed a personal prayer. It was written on the pages of my heart, a secret to myself. Then I returned to South India where my parents live. Before returning to the city, I went to see a friend and relative. She is a wonderful godly woman. Even though I visited her at midnight, she was delighted to see me. "This is the best time to meet since there is nobody to disturb us." I liked her attitude. We began to talk. I told her about my experience and then I said to her, "I came here just to be prayed for. Would you pray for me?" So she began to pray.

Then she said to me, "This is what you have been praying for. You have asked God for a sign. God has listened to that prayer and He says, 'I will give you the sign to let you know that it is I who has called you to ministry in this place.'

This is the sign God gives you. Three things will happen to you when you go back. A woman will come to you who has been diagnosed with cancer. Pray for her and I will make her well. A man will come in search of you. He will tell you that he has AIDS. Pray for him. I will heal him. Somebody will call on you to pray for a man on his deathbed. Go and pray for him and I will raise him up from his bed of illness." I was now more fearful than before. Cancer, AIDS, death bed, I thought to myself. I returned to my pastoral responsibility with fear and trembling but also with an excitement of what I was going to experience in the future.

A few months later I met one of the church members. I asked her how she was. "Well, I am not too good," the woman told me. "But this is the Christmas season! You should be excited," I told her. "Pastor, I have just come from the hospital. I have been diagnosed with cancer and the doctors have given me three to six months to live." I said to her, "Don't worry. Jesus can make you well." In my heart I wondered if this was the woman I had been told about. I was not too sure. She turned around and then said to me, "Pastor, pray for me." I assured her I would and with tears in her eyes she walked away from me. Just as she walked away, I heard a voice in my heart, *"My son, call her back. She thinks you are saying these things because this is the language of pastors. They need to speak like this in order to give hope to people. Tell her that it is not you who is speaking, I AM is speaking! Tell her, I will make her well."* I called the woman back and told her exactly what the "voice" had told me to say. She asked me to visit her in her home. I visited her and prayed for her but every time I prayed for her and returned she only grew worse. I could not believe it. Did I hear right from God? Was she the woman God would heal? Did I get into some kind of mess here? The questions kept haunting me. I prayed more fervently for her.

It was a Sunday and the woman's son approached me after the service and requested that I come to her home on that very day. He requested that I bring some oil and pray over his mother. He told me that it was time for her to go home to be with the Lord. I was discouraged that her condition had not improved. I promised him that I would come over.

It was at that time that my son David took seriously ill. When I was leaving home some friends in the church thought I was taking him to be admitted to the hospital. I told them I was going to pray for someone who was not well. I also told them that David's illness was only an attack of the devil. Seeing I was going about doing the Lord's work, He would surely take care of my son.

When I arrived at their home that evening there was a deadly silence. Every one of their relatives arrived at the house from different parts of the country as well as from overseas. They were expecting the inevitable. I stepped into the room where she was groaning in great agony. "I want to die. I can't bear the pain anymore." These were the words on her lips. I mentioned to her that if this was what she was going to say, my prayer for her would be useless and even the Lord would not be able to help her. I told her to ask God to forgive her, to tell Him, "I am ready for anything. If you want to heal me, heal me. If you want me to come home, I am ready." She sincerely lifted this prayer up to God. Then I told the family members that those who did not have faith to see a miracle must step outside of the room. Everyone else could stay. I applied oil over her forehead and cried out to God in a loud prayer of intercession. By the time we were through all of us were dripping with sweat and tears.

We went outside for some fresh air. No one talked. To break the silence I asked them to get the guitar I had found in their attic. I wiped the dust off and began to play some of the old favorites. I had barely played the third song when I saw her seated in the chair in front of me. I told her that she should rest and not strain herself. She told me that she heard the singing and desired to be there with the rest of us. I sang with the family for almost an hour. She continued to sit and be part of the gathering. A few days later, she went to the hospital to be examined. The physicians conducted the tests at least three times and concluded that the machines were working all right. The patient simply did not have any cancer in her body. Praise the Lord for the first sign. We were all excited to look forward to the future, expecting great things. That very night my son was also healed. We did not know that we were in for a double treat.

The Second Sign

WITH THE EXCITEMENT OF WHAT GOD DID BY HEAL-
ing a cancer patient, I began to share the story of my prayers
with people around me. Some young people in the church became really excited. Every time they met me they would ask,
"Did anybody with AIDS come to you?" "Not yet," I answered.
"What about somebody on a death bed?" "Not yet," I responded. So we lived in anticipation. One Saturday evening as we
were preparing for the Sunday worship service, the youth
gathered in the church for a time of Bible study and fellowship.

It was then I saw a man walk in to the church compound.
Someone told me, "There is a man looking for you," so I went
outside to meet him. I asked him who he was and who he
wanted to see. He told me that he had come to see the pastor. I told him I was the pastor and he gave me a strange look.
Maybe to him I did not look like a pastor. He said he would
come another time so I asked him, "Why don't you tell me
what you want and why you came now?" "Another time," he
said. I told him that I had time for him and encouraged him to
tell me how I could help. He hesitated but once again replied,
"No, no, another time." Suddenly I realized why he wanted to
come another time and said, "You don't want to talk right now
because you are drunk. Before I became a pastor I lived in the
world like you. I knew you the very moment I saw you." Then
he responded, "I'll come when I am sober."

I did not want to see this man leave. I wanted to be able to
help him. So, I continued, "I want to tell you, my friend, you
will never be sober. I do not mean to offend you, but if you
really wanted to be sober, you would be sober right now. You
are not able to be sober now because you don't have power
over your drinking habit. You do not have the power to be free.
Today I can introduce you to the Power that is greater than the
power that is at work in your life."

By this time he became very angry. I put my hands on him. He turned around and said, "Take your hands off me!" I asked him why he was so angry and assured him that I meant him no harm. "Take your hands off me right now!" he insisted. Once again I asked him why he was so upset and what was troubling him. He again insisted that I take my hands off him immediately. "Give me one reason and I will gladly take my hands off." He drew close to me and whispered in my ear, "I have AIDS." I realized that he was the man the Lord had talked to me about.

I embraced him and said to him, "I am an ordinary person, a sinner like you. But if Jesus was here He would have embraced you and He would have whispered in your ears how much He loves you, even at this moment." Before I could complete my sentence, he broke down and cried like a little boy. He said to me, "Sir, see this pathetic situation in which I am. in. I have been instrumental in starting Alcoholics Anonymous in various cities in India. I have traveled across the length and the breadth of this country. I have given speeches on the perils of drinking but look at me now. I am a drunk! Why? Because I live in fear every day! I know I will die of AIDS. I have had no one to talk to. You are young and you have many years to live." I said, "What makes you say that? Remember, no one is assured of life tomorrow. It could be that today is the last day for any one on this planet earth. You are afraid to die and I am not! Do you know why I am not afraid? Because I know what is going to happen to me. When I die I leave my physical body and walk into eternity with my new heavenly body, because I cannot take my physical body along with me. Technically, I do not die, I live. I will tell you how you can live too, if you will only allow me to." He said, "Sure sir." I responded, "I want to tell you of a God who loves you."

The man continued to tell me that when he found out he was infected with the AIDS virus his family threw him out of the house. After this happened he traveled like a vagabond over the entire country, not knowing what else to do. Today he knew he had traveled to the right place because on this day he intended to take his own life. As he walked along the street he heard a voice that said "Open this gate and go in." That is how he ended up in the church.

I decided to tell him that God had told me he would send someone who was infected with the AIDS virus. "Pray for him and I will make him well," God said. And so, I took him to the church, gave him a copy of the Bible, and showed him all the important passages of scripture. "For all the questions that I have had in my life the answers are found in this book. Thank you! Thank you!"

Then he continued expressing his desire to confess his sins. I encouraged him to confess them to a sinless Savior, not to me, a sinner saved by grace. At this I led him to the altar of our church. There he beat upon his chest so loud that I thought his ribs would crack. His cries were so loud I thought our roof would shake and shatter. He cried out with his heart to God. "Jesus forgive me, forgive this sinner." The young people who were there at the time quickly moved out of the church and prayed outside. After his confession, I led him to faith in Jesus Christ.

Many days later I received a note from him slipped under the door.

Sir, ever since I put my faith in Christ something has begun to happen in my life. I went back to the railroad station to get a ticket to go home. I did not have the money and there surprisingly, I met a friend of mine. He was so happy to see me but so surprised to see me in this condition. I told him of my experience. He quickly bought me a set of clothes and he put some money in my pocket for the train ticket and gave me some food to eat. I was on my way home.

When I arrived at my home, I told my wife and my daughter about the miracle that God had done. Thank you for reuniting me with my family. Through Jesus Christ I found hope. I am so encouraged and have lost any desire to drink. I feel well. Thank you for showing me the way to Jesus.

As much as he was excited, I was even more excited. I knew the third event was just around the corner for us to experience. Thank you Lord!

Call Her Lydia

THE YEAR 2001 WAS A REMARKABLE YEAR. IN THE BEginning of the year, I remember reading the Bible afresh for my personal devotional time. As I was reading Genesis 18:10 where the Lord speaks to Abraham, something strange happened.

"I will surely return to you about this time next year, and Sarah your wife will have a son," the verse states. The letters appeared to leap out of the pages of the Bible. With my physical eyes I was able to see the words in the Bible but at the same I saw the words that were lifted up supernaturally, the word "daughter" in the place of "son." In my heart I knew God was going to bless us with a daughter that year.

On March 10, 2001, I was sitting in a Bible Study group that gathered in the home of Mr. C. P. John. Mr. John Khushal was teaching from Acts 16 on the life of Lydia. It was around 7:30 p.m. when I heard the voice of God. "My son, you will have a daughter. Give her the name, Lydia!" I was surprised.

On the way back home I shared my experience with Angie. We prayed and thanked God. The next day, Mr. Solomon, who came to help me in the church office, asked me what God had been teaching me lately. I innocently shared my experience of the previous night. As you might imagine, the news spread to all the members of the Church that the Pastor's family is going to have a baby. More specifically, this baby will be a daughter and God had told our pastor that he would have to call her Lydia. I was terrified. What a predicament! From that day on, I prayed earnestly to God, that we would have a daughter. What would people think of me if Angie had a son?

On August 15 of that year, Angie became hypertensive and collapsed in the university where she had been teaching. At the time, I was in another city speaking at a church retreat. I returned back to the city to learn that Angie had been hospitalized. Due to complications with her pregnancy, the doctors encouraged me to abort the baby and not take the chance of losing my wife. Deep in my heart I knew God had other plans. I believed nothing could go wrong because God was in control. I prayed to God and he spoke to me through Isaiah 66:9. *"Do I bring to the moment of birth and not give delivery? Do I close up the womb when I bring to delivery?"* I was greatly encouraged.

After the many trials that we went through during this period, God continued to give me assurances that things would be all right. The Lord told me Lydia would be a joy and delight to me in my old age. Later on I realized that this was the very prophecy the angel had uttered to Zechariah concerning John the Baptist. That is the beauty of hearing from the Lord. It provides you supernatural strength when you need to face frightening situations in life. God's word is always greater and more powerful than our circumstances.

During this time, our church was preparing for a praise and worship concert. This was the first time we were attempting to have four different churches from four different denominations in the city come together. The members of the choir asked me to postpone or cancel the event because of Angie's health. I told them that we must worship God in this situation. The choir members then decided that after our final rehearsal they would sing to Angie at the hospital during the evening hours.

What an experience it turned out to be! Such wonderful hearts and voices surrounded her bed in worship to the Lord. Her spirits were lifted up. The next day, however, singing and worshipping God became a challenge. That night I struggled to hold back the tears as we sang, "God is good all the time."

Angie faced many problems during this term but the Lord brought us through each one. Angie did experience further complications and God gave more assurances from Isaiah 66:7. *"Before she goes into labor, she gives birth; before the pains come upon her, she delivers a son."* I wondered how that could possibly happen. Later I realized that God was trying to let me know Angie was going to have a Caesarian section! On the 20th day of October 2001, our Lydia was born. We celebrated her birth with our entire church family. What a joy she has been to us ever since! I pray that like Lydia of the book of Acts, our Lydia will be available for God to use in anyway He chooses.

The Third Sign

IN AUGUST OF 1997 THE LORD GAVE THE PROMISE OF A third sign to me. A year and a half went by. Two of the signs had already taken place. As I continued yet another day as the pastor of the Lal Bagh Methodist Church in the city of Lucknow, so many questions and challenges stood before me. I wondered if I was truly the shepherd of these people?

In an effort to find answers, I examined myself in the light of God's word. I looked within and arrived at some hard conclusions; I was inadequate to do the job; I lacked a Shepherd's heart; I did not have the passion to serve the Lord; and I did not have the excitement of even being a Christian.

I knew Lal Bagh Methodist Church had a great reputation. It had produced many bishops for the Methodist Church. But, when would I see the longings of my heart fulfilled? And, was I the person to lead?

I had just finished another day at the church office when I received a phone call. The woman caller told me that she was calling on behalf of her family and wondered if I could possibly come over to their home and pray for her dad who was not well? They were not members of our congregation the caller told me. She explained that her dad had taken ill and was now in a coma. While the conversation was going on, I felt that *maybe* this was the third miracle. In my heart I felt God telling me to go and visit this sick man and his family. I had the assurance that God would raise a man from his deathbed and told her that I would come that evening.

Angie and I arrived at their home which was situated not too far from the church. As we entered the room, I realized that they had practically turned the room where the father was in bed into a private hospital room. Monitors and tubes connected him to medical equipment. My heart sank. The family told us that the doctors had given up hope for his recovery. I knew the man was in critical condition.

When I saw his situation, many questions filled my mind. I had preached about faith that is essential for healing. But how could a man in this condition even know I was standing in front of him? How could he have enough faith to receive a miracle? Whose faith was going to make him well? Suddenly fear gripped me. This would be the first time I ever prayed for someone who was in a coma.

Many theological questions erupted in my mind. Even though I did not find the answers, the process challenged my paradigm of understanding God. I stood motionless. I needed more time. I requested that Angie sing a few songs while I was deciding exactly what I was going to do. I needed to prepare my heart for what God wanted me to know and understand. Angie asked the family what kind of songs their dad liked. Angie began to lead in singing those songs. *What a friend we have in Jesus*, we sang together. While they were singing, I prayed and asked God to show me how to pray for the man.

When we had finished singing the songs, I told the family that I was about to pray. Meanwhile, the Lord reminded me about the authority He had given me. I found it natural to operate as a child of God, pleading for the mercy and blessing of God. However, I found it difficult to operate with authority as a servant of God. The Lord reminded me it was indeed a delegated authority. So I mustered enough courage and prayed in a loud voice, *In the name of Jesus, the name that is above every name in heaven and earth and under the earth and in the authority God has given to me as His servant, I speak to this body: Respond to the name of Jesus!*

Before the prayer was even completed, the man suddenly sat up on his bed. When I heard the sound, in utter shock and amazement, I opened my eyes. There was a twinkle in his eyes and with a smile on his face he focused his eyes on me and said, "You are Rev. Moses, aren't you?" I responded with a smile. Then he looked at Angie and said, "You are Mrs. Moses, aren't you?" She smiled as well.

Meanwhile the family had realized that their loved one was back to normal. He was able to recognize people, able to speak and able to hear as well. They could not contain their emotions. With a loud outburst of joy and happiness they embraced the man. I realized it was a special moment for the whole family and asked them if Angie and I could be excused so that we could be on our way home. I did not make it further than the parking lot in front of the house when one of his daughters came running toward us. "Pastor Moses, have you ever seen anything like this ever before in your life?" I said to her, "With God, all things are possible."

This was the third sign that God had promised me to let me know that He had called me to this city to be a Methodist pastor and that He would always be with me. I knew that this was the beginning of my great adventure with God, an adventure that would never cease. It can only get bigger and better. The call of God on my life today is to let the whole world know that Jesus has no equals, no competition and that there is none like Him. I thank God for the sign, a sign of many good things to come.

The Train Journey

BROUGHT UP IN SOUTH INDIA, I FOUND HINDI EX-tremely difficult to learn. Hindi is the local language spoken by most of the people in Lucknow. Among all the challenges I faced in ministry, I longed to share the gospel with people and lead them to faith in Jesus Christ. The ability to speak the language was important.

But, I also knew that I was struggling because of my poor health. At the slightest trouble I faced, I cried to God and asked Him if He would help me. There were times I even wanted to escape the challenging ministry of being a pastor. I wished there were other options that could make life a lot easier.

With crowded schedules, days and weeks seemed to pass by rapidly. When the summer set in I longed to go home to South India for my annual vacation. The train journey has never been comfortable. I dreaded the travel and at the same time I was excited to meet my family, friends and relatives and share with them my burden to reach North India with the gospel. I also enjoyed sharing the new things God was doing in my life.

As I was about to take the annual trip down to South India one summer, I was busy making arrangements for lay leaders of the church to take care of the ministry in my absence. When I approached my immediate superiors to approve my leave, I met with several obstacles. Angie and the children had already taken the trip a couple of weeks earlier, as they could afford a longer vacation. When my chances of sorting out things and making the trip looked bleak, I rushed to a last minute appoint-ment with the Bishop to consider my leave of absence from the church. To my delight, the Bishop was understanding and told me I could take the leave I had requested. I rushed back to the parsonage before dashing off to the railroad station to make the long and tedious journey.

It was hot that summer. The outside temperature climbed to between 42 and 45 degrees centigrade (108 to 113 F)! Knowing that there was no seat available for me in the air-conditioned coach, I was mentally prepared to travel. I was happy just to get to the railroad station on time. *Lord, I am thankful for being able to travel to Chennai again. You know I do not feel well in my body. I know you can control the weather and make this trip a pleasant one. I ask that you would help me to rest and have a peaceful trip. Please help me to remain silent and not be disturbed by the other passengers on this train.* I bid goodbye to my friend Pandian, who came to see me off at the train station. I was ready for the more than 40-hour journey.

Barely had the train left the station in Lucknow, when I noticed a woman reclining in the narrow seat in front me. She seemed very sick and needing immediate medical assistance. I wondered if she was even going to make it through the long train journey that was in front of us. With a feeble voice she gently asked if I could exchange the window seat I had with her. She appeared to need the window seat and the fresh air it would provide her. Seeking the silence and rest my body needed and to avoid any further conversation with her, I immediately gave into her request. She was delighted with the offer.

As she moved into the new seat by the window, she asked me why I had given up my seat so willingly. I told her not to make much of it and that I was only glad to help. However, my curiosity got the better of me. Looking at her frail frame, I asked her if she was unwell and why she was taking such a hazardous journey when she was aware of her medical condition. She told me that she was returning home. Now I was even more curious. I wanted to know the reason for her travels in North India. She replied, "I had to take the journey since I am getting old." I was surprised. "What has age got to do with travel in the north?" She replied, "Son, it is all because of my sins!"

I could not resist asking what she had done to account for her sins. Obviously frustrated over the experience, the woman told me her story.

"I know I am getting old and advancing in years. I am aware that I do not have much time left. So I desired to get rid of the many sins I had committed in my life. This is why I am part of this group of devotees traveling on this train. We have traveled

together for over two weeks to the most holy and sacred Hindu pilgrimage centers in North India. Just like my companions, I have dipped myself in the sacred rivers of India to have my sins washed away. With great difficulty I have climbed innumerable steep and rugged steps in the mountainside, where these sacred temples are located in order to see the deities and offer my prayers to them. I am also extremely upset that our tour guide did not provide me enough time and opportunity to gaze upon the gods and goddesses there. The organizers are only after my money!"

After listening to her story, I could not help but ask her if her sins had been forgiven. "I am not sure!" Again I could not resist asking her how much money she had spent going on this pilgrimage. When she told me it had cost her Rs.14,000 which is equivalent to $312 U.S., I was astounded. I assured her that if she would give me five minutes, I would tell her how her sins could be forgiven with no cost to her, free of charge! She eagerly accepted my proposition. I shared my life story with her and told her how Jesus came to this world for the purpose of dying on the cross for our sins. I let her know how the price had already been paid and that if she received the salvation that Jesus offered with a child-like faith, then she could enjoy peace with God. "You can become a child of God," I said with a smile, "and God will be your heavenly Father."

She was simply overjoyed to hear this good news. Suddenly she was no longer thinking of the time. She even seemed to have forgotten her sickness. Her face beamed with happiness. I was also overjoyed at the opportunity the Lord had granted me to share my faith with someone on the train that day. But now I was ready to seek the elusive silence and the much-needed rest for my body that I had looked forward to during the long journey.

As usual, God had other plans! The old woman now was no longer as sick as she appeared earlier. Her enthusiasm overflowed. She immediately got the attention of her fellow passengers who were seated in the same section of our train compartment. She insisted that they needed to hear all the things I had shared with her earlier. Instead of the silence I had longed for, I was enjoying the opportunity to share my faith in Christ with several ladies. They were openly amazed and receptive to the Gospel.

As I tried to get back to that much-deserved and needed rest, I realized the old woman was not giving up spreading her enthusiasm to passengers on the train and had managed to get another six passengers to exchange their seats with those who already heard what I had to say. I was amazed by the sequence of events as well as the ongoing experience. It seemed that as much as I desired to go out to fish, the fish were jumping into my pond! Inwardly I could not stop thanking God for the unusual event that I was experiencing, while simultaneously crying out to God in intercessory prayer that lives would be touched and blessed with salvation through Jesus Christ.

No sooner had I finished spending time with a new group of passengers, when the old woman was making plans for another group to come into our compartment. Before too long I realized we had moved into the late hours of the night. I asked the old woman how she was able to have such a great influence over their lives. She replied that she had come to know them just recently but was sure that, like her, they would also be unsure of their salvation even after making this holy pilgrimage to various parts of North India. I could hardly believe my ears as she spoke of their spiritual thirst and their sense of being lost.

The next day was almost a repeat of the previous day's experience. Since the train journey took between 42 to 45 hours, I had all the time in the world to share my faith, without even having to move an inch from my seat! The joy of sharing my faith in Jesus Christ seemed to have caused the tiredness and fatigue in my physical body to disappear. In fact, I felt as if I had been given a supernatural strength that allowed me to relentlessly talk with passion about what Jesus could do for each one of them. The hours of the day seemed like fleeting seconds. By the end of the second evening on the train, I concluded there were no more passengers left in the compartment that had not heard about Jesus. As the second night came, I profusely thanked God for this incredible opportunity to share Jesus and the resulting joy I experienced in the process. I slipped into a restful night with praises to God on my lips. I knew I still had almost half of the following day to rest. I would spend it in silence until I reached my destination - the city of Chennai. I was hopeful that things would turn out as I planned, at least during the last leg of the 2,100 kilometers (1,260 miles) long train journey.

Whoops! I was wrong again! Once again, God had other plans. As I sipped my tea and allowed the fresh breeze to whiz past my head, a young woman suddenly appeared. Even before telling me her story, her eyes filled with tears. She told me she could not resist coming over to talk to me—even though she was concerned that people might misunderstand if she was seen with me in her emotional state—after all that she had heard from others. She told me how the other passengers in the compartment were talking about a man who had shared his faith in Jesus and how salvation through Jesus was such a simple plan of God. She then asked me if I had time for her and whether she could share something personal with me. Without hesitating, I asked her to take a seat and tell me her story. What I heard made my heart sink with utter shock and sadness. This was her story.

"Sir, I am the worst sinner in the company of all the passengers in this compartment. I am the leader of the entire group that is returning home from the pilgrimage. In fact, I am their tour guide. When I heard them discussing the things that you had shared I could not wait any longer. I don't think I can forgive myself. I cried for the sin I have committed by being their tour guide. Let me confess something to you. I was born in a Hindu family. At a very young age I had an opportunity to hear the gospel of Jesus Christ. I was overjoyed with the gift of salvation Jesus offered me free of charge. With such excitement and passion I shared my newfound faith with others. The days were exciting. But the nights were a different experience altogether. My parents soon realized I was reading the Bible and was disinterested in the family prayers offered to idols. They threatened me with dire consequences. I did not know what to do. Being a girl, I knew I would be ostracized from our community and worse still, I would be thrown out of my home. It did not take long before the worst thing I had imagined took place. One night, after an intense argument with my family, I was forced to leave home and all links with my close-knit family were gone. But, I still had strong convictions that enabled me to walk with the Lord.

"It did not take much time to realize that the Christian community could not help a discarded Hindu convert for too long. Now I was left with nowhere to go. I did not have a future. I knew no

one would marry me in this situation. I became desperate. After living a comfortable life I could not adjust to the hardships of life. It was at this time I met a young man with whom I shared my life story. He was not a Christian but he was very understanding. I knew I had found someone who loved me in spite of all that I had been through. I knew that I was getting into a relationship that the Bible declared as forbidden. I also knew I was left with no choice but to get into something rather than be lonely and uncertain in life. The relationship gradually led into our marriage.

"Suddenly things became drastically different. My husband began to accuse me of not providing for my family. I was not used to hard work. We ended each night in arguments. He blamed me for everything that went wrong in our relationship. Now our differences were about our religious beliefs. Our conversations ended in conflicts. He had a bad temper that left me beaten up, bruised and abused. His previously rare outbursts became a common feature. I knew I could not endure it any longer. So I tried to pick up any job that came my way. People made promises but I could never find a decent job. It was at that time I found an opening to be a tour guide. I thought it would take me away for days and weeks from my abusive husband. Before I even started working this new job my husband threw me out of our home. Now I was left to fend for myself. I needed the job very badly.

"I thought this position was something that could give me a chance to travel, have a change and make some decent money too. But the work I had to perform was contrary to my faith. It created a great anguish in my heart. I knew that I was expected to lead people to different locations on a sacred pilgrimage to find forgiveness for their sins and experience solace in their hearts. While I did my job, deep inside I felt like a hypocrite most of the time. Did anyone know that I, being the tour guide, was in fact the one who knew the answer to their spiritual thirst? What if they knew I had tasted it myself? Would they rise up in anger if they knew that I had been unwilling and reluctant to share the truth with them? How would they feel if they knew that I, knowing all these truths, had led them to take the strenuous climb up those mountains? How could I take them there to gaze on these lifeless gods?

"Sir, my heart is broken within me. If I tell them the truth, I will probably lose my job. I am only going along with this because I need the money so desperately. Sir, who will understand me? Will Jesus forgive me? What can I do now?"

As the tears continued to flow, I assured her that if there was anyone who could understand her and still be willing to forgive her, it was Jesus. She was astonished to hear that. I told her that she needed to confess her sins in order to experience forgiveness in her heart. I also reminded her that forgiveness includes the desire to forsake the sin as well. I told her that she needed to believe that God would grant her a better job, not necessarily a better salary package.

With tears running down her cheeks, she confessed her sin and received forgiveness. I could see the joy of the Lord on her face immediately. I encouraged her to put her trust in the Lord and allow the Lord to guide her life. What a finish to a long train journey! I wondered how and where the two days had gone.

The Spirit of the Lord refreshed me. I jokingly said to someone after the incident was over, "My two days of ministry was sponsored completely by the Indian Railways!" Praise the Lord for his mysterious ways in our lives.

Prayer Partners

BY NOW I HAD SPENT ALMOST THREE YEARS IN THE Lal Bagh Methodist Church as the Pastor. It was during this time that I met someone from the United States, who eventually became a friend.

This woman was a friend of one of our church members, Snehalata David, and came to the city in order to conduct prayer seminars to challenge people to participate in prayer for the salvation of India. The prayer conference was conducted in the building adjacent to our church. As the conference was taking place on the church campus, I decided to quietly slip in to enjoy the benefit of being in the company of those who had come together for prayer.

As the meeting got underway, Kathleen Dillard was delivering the session on prayer. I had always had a keen interest in learning more about the deep things of prayer. Throughout all my growing years as a Christian I had been associated with men and women of God who were giants in their prayer life. I did not want to lose a learning opportunity that morning.

Casually attired with a T-shirt and jeans I sneaked in through the rear entrance hoping the participants there would not notice me. But to my surprise, Kathleen stopped her teaching session abruptly. She motioned toward me and with her hand indicated that I should come to the front. I felt embarrassed but reluctantly walked right through the crowd and made my way to the front. The whole group, which was watching and listening with rapt attention to her teaching, now turned their attention on me.

When Snehalata's husband saw me, he informed Kathleen that I was their pastor. Kathleen continued by posing a question to me. "Have you seen me before?" she asked.

"No! I have never seen you nor have I met you."

"Obviously, you have not met me before. But I have seen you!"

I disagreed with her and wanted to know when that took place since I knew we had never seen or met before. In front of all the participants Kathleen Dillard said, "I saw you at 4:30 a.m. this morning!"

I asked her how that could possibly be true since I knew where I was at that time that morning.

Then she told me about something fascinating she had experienced.

She had booked herself into a hotel not very far from the church campus and...

"This morning while I was praying to God about the conference in the early hours of the morning something different happened. God brought your face in front of me during the time of prayer. He told me that you were the pastor of this church and you were in the church early this morning at 4.30 a.m. You were spending time with God even as you were walking and praying at the same time. Was that true?" With a surprised look on my face I said, "Yes." She continued, *"God said to me, 'Pray for this man. He needs much prayer. He is praying that he needs prayer partners who could support him in prayer. Pray for him.' "* So she said, "I do not know anything about you but I want to tell you that since I have been commanded by God, I will pray for you from this day. I have prayer partners all across the world. At least forty of them pray for me every day by name. They pray specifically for my family and the work that I do in various places. I will let them know that from today they will need to pray for you as well since I have been commanded by Jesus to pray for you." On hearing this I broke down in front of all of them and wept. Why? Because whenever people asked me, "what can I do for you?" I have always replied, "The best thing that you can ever do for me is to pray for me. Without your prayer support, nothing much can be accomplished in this place." I said to the Lord, "Thank you for answering this prayer request. Thank you for granting me people who will pray for me so that the ministry that you have called me to do can be powerful and effective."

It was amazing to know how the Lord raised prayer partners for me across the world. Thank you Jesus!

Spirit Invade Me

I REALIZE THAT AT DIFFERENT POINTS IN MY LIFE, GOD has inspired me to write songs. It is amazing when I also realize that I cannot read music and don't even know much about music.

As a boy, I learned to play the guitar the hard way. I enrolled for guitar classes that cost me 20 rupees a month, which is approximately 40 cents U.S. My family could not afford to spend that much money at that time. One day before setting out for the class, I told my dad that I could not go to class since the teacher would expect me to make the payment. My dad told me that he did not have the money that day. I decided to skip the class, but my father insisted that I should go. So I took my guitar and went anyway.

My teacher said, "So you have forgotten to bring the money!"

I apologized to him saying, "I forgot."

I did not want him to know my family situation so I assured him I would make the payment the following day. To my dismay he told me to leave the guitar with him and return home to bring the monthly fee. Even though I decided to quit taking the lessons, my teacher did not allow me to take my guitar home. I was furious and cried all the way home.

As I told my parents what had happened, my father assured me that he would go with me and talk to my teacher. The moment my teacher saw my dad, he said, "Uncle, how are you? Why did you come? This is not a big deal. I told your son that he could always pay me later." I was shocked! Did I mention that my teacher was a Christian? He certainly was not acting like it. Now, I did not even want to be a Christian. I thought Christians were nothing but hypocrites.

So I lost the opportunity to learn to play and watched when others played, hoping that someday I could play the guitar and sing at the same time like them. Then God helped me. I began strumming, singing and using the guitar in worship as well as for my own benefit.

One day I had just come back to the parsonage after attending the Methodist Day that falls on January 7th every year. By this time, I had been the Pastor of the Lal Bagh Methodist Church for about three years. It was biting cold that day. Hailing from the south of India, I found it extremely cold and clothed myself with every possible woolen outfit I could find. But, it was the events of the day — not the cold — that filled my thoughts and disturbed me no end.

We had gathered together on the campus of the famous Lucknow Christian College established by the Methodist Mission. The Bishop of the Methodist Church, the various pastors of the Lucknow Regional Conference of the Methodist Church in India and many lay leaders representing the churches congregated to celebrate the occasion.

Many people came up to the platform to talk about the beginnings of Methodism under the dynamic leadership of the renowned Rev. John Wesley. A passing reference was made to the "Aldersgate" experience of John Wesley and how his heart was strangely warmed on the night of May 24, 1738. Then the achievements of both Rev. William Butler and Rev. William Taylor were presented for their outstanding contribution to the Methodist Church in India.

Mention was made of the "Methodist Trail," which was about the tremendous preaching and great responses as they established the Methodist Mission. Churches, schools, colleges, hospitals and a publishing house of great reputation sprouted up all over the face of North India. There was much appreciation from the esteemed gathering of church leaders. The celebration ended with refreshments and a cup of Indian *chai* [tea]. Since the weather conditions were extreme, I held the warm cup of chai in my hand to generate heat to my body that felt like it was nearly freezing and wondered about the symbol of the Methodist Church, a cross and a flame. Pondering over this I returned home.

My heart continued to reel under the effects of what I had felt throughout the day. With the temperature not improving, I stayed indoors. The same old questions returned to haunt me. Lord, have you stopped doing such things like those you did during John Wesley's time? Will these things ever happen during my lifetime? Should I rethink and understand the Bible differently? Has the power of God seen and experienced by the people of the Bible and in Church history diminished? Is there something drastically wrong in my life that is hindering me from seeing and experiencing these things?

My heart cried out in desperation to God. As the night approached, we sat together as a family at the table. When the dinner was over, I asked my family to go to bed while I decided to stay at the table. Tears continued to flow down my cheeks.

As midnight approached, my heart began to receive the words that eventually became a song. This song is a prayer from a desperate heart.

Spirit Invade Me

Spirit invade me
Set my heart ablaze for Thee
Spirit invade me
Set my heart on fire for Thee
For without you my life is like a candle
Without you my life is like a candle without a flame

Chorus
For without you
The sun will have no sunshine
And the moon will have no glow
For without you, without you
The clouds will have no rain
And the river will have no flow

For without you
The rainbow will lose its color
And the bud will refuse to bloom
For without you, without you
The page will have no letter
And the music will have no tune

For without you
The face will lose its laughter
And the heart its power to love
For without you, without you
Man won't know his future
Or where he came from

For without you
The Father will be a myth
And the cross will have no Son
For without you, without you
The Church will have no Spirit
And this song will remain unsung.

The Holy Communion

ONCE AGAIN, SUNDAY MORNING HAD ARRIVED! AS A pastor, the weekdays seemed to quickly fly by and before I realized what had taken place, Sunday seemed to await me again.

By this time God had developed a great prayer life for me. It is a simple secret - more problems...more prayer! God had also placed in my heart a passion to preach on the need to practice holiness in our lives. Each day I could be found in the church at approximately 4:30 a.m. spending time talking to God about my personal life as well as praying for the concerns of the Church.

This particular morning I was in the church at the usual time. Since it was a Sunday morning I also knew I had to rehearse my sermon and get the order of the worship service finalized as soon as possible. I looked at my watch and it showed exactly 4:30 a.m. Unlocking the doors of the church, I entered through the side entrance and walked to the main altar area.

As a matter of practice, I walked away from the main altar area to the rear end of the church where the main entrance was located. Then, turning around I would begin the prayer time and announce to the Lord that I had come to spend time with Him in prayer. I would run through the long list I had prepared to set forth before Him for His favorable considerations.

Looking back, I felt I had set the agenda for the meeting I had planned with God. I would pray from there before gradually moving closer to the altar area. Then kneeling before God, I would commit myself to His service. Then I would lift up the congregation and the different needs of the people to God and finally finish the prayer time. As I was about to embark on this usual practice in prayer, I had a strange and unusual experience. It started when I heard the familiar voice of God speaking to me.

My son, turn around. I was trembling in fear and thought to myself, what is there to see at this time of day, Lord? It is pitch dark and I know the church lights are not on. Nevertheless I obeyed God's voice.

To my utter shock, I saw people kneeling at the altar! What a strange sight. To be honest, I was terrified. How could anyone enter the church at this odd hour of the day? Who are these people I wondered. What are they doing at the altar?

I knew I was seeing a vision from the Lord. I stood speechless and motionless. Then the voice of the Lord came to me again. *My son, get close to the altar and look at them. You know them!*

By then I was terrified so I tiptoed with fear towards the altar. As I looked at their faces I did recognize them. Again the Lord spoke to me. *These people come to me but their hearts are far away. I want you to tell them what I have told you.*

I immediately dropped on my knees and began to cry. I said, "Lord, who am I that I should do all these things? I only expected to be a simple pastor and desired an insignificant life. I am not like the prophets of the Bible. I do not have the courage to do all these things."

In a stern voice God quickly replied to my concerns. *My son, if you want to be my servant, do what I tell you.*

I pleaded with the Lord. I bargained with Him. I wished there was some other way of doing it. I asked God to help me and told Him that I would do as he had asked but on one condition. I would not tell their names. With that done I begged God to forgive me.

Quickly I prayed for the many other concerns of the church and returned back to the parsonage. I sat in the church office, picked up my Bible and began to read. I could not concentrate on the sermon and put my thoughts together. I cried to God for help.

In a short while the Sunday worship service was underway. We spent some time worshipping the Lord with songs and music. Then I led in the pastoral intercessory prayer. We felt the divine presence of God in our midst and now the time had come for the sermon.

As I started, I shared with the congregation the vision that the Lord showed me early that morning during my time of prayer. You could hear a pin drop in the church. I told the congregation that the Lord had given me a word for them early this morning during my prayer time. Here is what I told them:

"At 4.30 a.m., while I was here in the church for prayer, the Lord showed me people kneeling at the altar. I trembled in fear not knowing who these people were. It was then that the Lord told me that I knew them. He asked me to go close to the altar to see their faces. The Lord told me that these people come to Him but their hearts are far away from Him. "

At this point, I began to cry and pleaded for the people to repent of their sins and get right with God. It was a tremendous feeling. I went on to tell them that at the end of the service we were going to kneel at the same altar to remember the body and blood of the Lord Jesus Christ who died for us. Again I pleaded with them to get right with God.

By the end of the sermon, I could see many lacked the courage to walk to the altar for communion. Some came with obvious fear. I saw many a hand tremble as I administered the sacraments of the Lord's Supper. In silence people returned to their seats for more prayer and self-examination. I trembled as I led the service and prayed the prayer of consecration. The usual laughter and fellowship over some light refreshments after the service was missing as people silently left the church and made their way to their homes.

Throughout the week the telephone kept ringing. The callers all wondered if they were the person the Lord had shown to the Pastor? Even as I walked the streets of the city and in the market place, the questions were the same. "Was it I?"

I could discern the fear in their faces. The Lord did something amazing in that Sunday worship service. He enabled many people to get right with God. I praise God for the many lives that were touched and transformed on that day. It was indeed a Holy Communion with God.

Commanding the Angels

IN THE YEAR 2000, I HOSTED A PRAYER SEMINAR CONducted by Dr. T.C. Fomum at the Lal Bagh Methodist Church. After the one-day seminar in Lucknow, there was a three-day conference in Allahabad. I was so impressed with this man of God, the challenges he faced and the miracles God performed in his life, that I became so energized and was ready to go. We spent the whole day in prayer, seeking the face of God. It was there that I met Kathleen and Snehalata, who were at the meeting as well. That night, we got together for prayer.

During the prayer time, Kathleen told me that God had told her that He had given me His authority to do His work. She encouraged me to not be afraid to use His authority in ministry. From now on she continued, "people will come to you when you call them to attempt something for the Lord. Soon people will recognize that authority in you and respect you for it."

From that point on, I began to search the Scriptures and was surprised to see how God delegated His authority to His disciples. These ordinary disciples did extraordinary things in His name. What they reported back after their ministry venture was nothing but the replication of what Jesus did! However, it was difficult for me to put myself in that position of being a disciple who exercised authority in the name of Jesus. It was one thing for me to read about it in Scripture but it was totally another thing to believe it and practice it in my life. I shuddered at the thought.

Kathleen told me, "Go back to your city. God has given you authority. Exercise it."

I thought about it many times but never had the courage to do it. I concluded every prayer with 'In the name of Jesus' formula. Did I really see that name as one of authority? Or was it a mere Christian formality?

One morning, around 4.30 a.m., I left the parsonage and entered the church to spend time with the Lord in prayer. All the lights were turned off and I was ready to get into a time of prayer. As I approached the altar from the side entrance, I said, "Jesus, I have come to spend time with you in prayer. Help me Lord! Give me a spirit of prayer. Teach me how to pray."

As I stood there ready to embark on a time of prayer, I heard a clear voice, *"My son, look up."* I had heard this voice several times before. Once again, I knew it was the Lord who was speaking to me. I began to cry for I knew this would be the greatest experience I could ever have in this world, to hear the voice of God.

I lifted my face and looked up not knowing what awaited me. To my utter shock, I saw two things. I saw the dark side of the roof of the church and the moon lit night sky. The sky was peppered generously with twinkling stars. I wondered how someone could possibly see the sky through the roof. It was incredible and beyond my comprehension.

Still adrift in bewilderment, a huge door appeared in the sky, far away in the distance. It was massive, the biggest door I had ever seen. As I was trying to make sense of it all, the massive door swung open. From that opening in the door, the largest flight of winding stairs I had ever seen descended. The stairs looked like they were reaching from heaven to earth. Lost in awe and wonder, I saw supernatural beings. These seemed like human figures draped in white garments and bathed in brilliant dazzling white. They were innumerable, maybe several thousand and descended from above in a synchronized manner. I saw light and brightness emanate from each one of them. I could not understand this incredible experience. Again, I heard the familiar voice of the Lord, *"My son, I have given you authority. Command these angels."*

Every day I had prayed that God would send His angels to fight His battles. I knew that angels were real beings assigned by God for every believer. I knew one of their responsibilities was to minister to God's servants. However, I felt small when I pondered over these spiritual matters. I began to shudder in fear. "Who am I that I should command the angels of God? No! Lord, I cannot do this. I am unworthy to do this." I began to find excuses. I wished I did not have to do these "unusual" things.

Then the Lord said to me in a deep and stern voice, *"My son, if you want to be my servant, do as I command you."* Now I knew I had no options left.

With much fear in my heart, I said, "In the name of Jesus, the name that is above every name in heaven and on earth and under the earth, and in the authority that God has granted to me as His servant, I command you angels of God. Go to the North!"

You understand that I was practicing spiritual warfare all throughout the season commanding the angels, begging God to send angels to protect this church from politics, from division, from formality and dead religion, from whatever is preventing us from experiencing excitement in Jesus and the life He promised.

That day God helped me to see what I believed was literally taking place. Could a word that is spoken by a mere mortal like me have such a profound effect? I saw divine supernatural beings do the bidding, North, South, East and West. A host of angels moved at a single command! Incredible! I am not sure of their hierarchy but they went in such huge numbers on hearing the command. I knew that God had indeed given me spiritual authority in the supernatural realm. I had seen it and experienced it.

Since then, I practice it every day in prayer and in ministry. It has had such results that seem even hard to believe. Without being aware of this authority, without practicing it in our spiritual lives, we cannot fight our spiritual battles. How then, can we experience victories in the many challenges we face in life? How else can we exalt the name of Jesus the Victor? No wonder Jesus told the Centurion who recognized the authority in Jesus, *"I have never found such faith in all Israel."* He not only recognized the authority of Jesus, the Centurion saw Him as THE AUTHORITY!

A Taste of Revival

I REMEMBER THE SPECIFIC DATE, MARCH 20, 2005. IT was 5:30 in the morning.

I had already finished my prayer time in the church. Coming out of the church, I walked around and saw a log of wood. I sat down and began to pray again. I began to visualize what God could do in answer to prayer. Then I heard His familiar voice again, *My son, you are crying and praying for a revival. If I would start a revival, are you ready to handle it?*

"No, Lord, we would not know how to handle it. We do not have the leaders to guide the huge numbers of people who would come in. We are not ready to teach people the ways of God. We are just not ready. It takes many people to be ready to bring in the harvest."

The Lord said to me, *Today I am going to give you a taste of revival.*

Today! I was so excited! I knew something was going to happen. I ran back to the parsonage and quickly penned down some points for the sermon that I was going to preach that morning. I shared this with Angie. I could not contain my anticipation. I knew God could work in spite of me.

I do not remember all the points that I preached that day, but it was a simple Methodist message. It contained just three points. The first one was from Acts 8. Philip was sent to the Ethiopian eunuch to help him in his spiritual quest for the truth. I described him as a man with an honorable intention to woreship in Jerusalem. The Ethiopian eunuch was a man reading the Scripture while returning from worshipping God. Tragedy of tragedies! The eunuch didn't know the God he had gone to worship. He asked Philip, "Who is this man whom the prophet Isaiah is referring to?" as he was pondering over Isaiah. God had sent Philip to enlighten his heart from the Scripture to point him to Jesus. Even before they had finished their discourse, the course of the Ethiopian's life was changed forever. He had the Scripture in his lap but no Savior in his heart!

Changed on the inside he said, "What hinders me from being baptized?" As I finished my first point, "Scripture in his lap but no Savior in his heart," I saw people breaking down and crying. I realized something important was happening and said, "Wait a minute. I have hardly finished my first point but these people seem ready to be saved!"

I pressed on to the next point found in John 7:37-39. On the last and greatest day of the Feast, Jesus stood and said in a loud voice, *"If anyone is thirsty, let him come to me and drink. Whoever believes in me, as the Scripture has said, streams of living water will flow from within him."*

Jesus knew that on the last day of the great festival, the people would go home disappointed because they were empty on the inside. They didn't need rituals. They needed an overflowing relationship with God. I remember preaching on that one too. I saw more people breaking down and crying. I cannot recall the third point in the message. The morning worship service was such an emotional experience. In the end, we sang, "Amazing grace, how sweet the sound" as many people responded to the invitation to repent of their sins and receive Christ as their Savior. My heart knew no bounds with the joy of the Lord that flooded my heart.

I hurried to finish the traditional way of greeting people as they left the church. As I returned I could see that many people were still sitting in their seats. Most of them were in tears and in prayer. I sat beside them and helped them to put their faith in Jesus Christ. I heard some astonishing confessions!

"Pastor, I have been a horrible sinner. I want to give up my sin."

"For too long I have been a hypocrite. I want to stop pretending."

"I have been running from God. I want to quit running."

"I know I am a sinner and I am ready to confess my sins."

"I need Him. Tell me how I can receive Christ."

The confessions went on and on and one after the other I prayed along with them. The worship service started at 9.00 a.m. in the morning. Normally we concluded at 11.00 a.m. But today, when I finished praying with them individually it was

4:00 p.m. What a great privilege to have a taste of revival! If this is a taste of revival, then I want the entire banquet.

My heart has longed for that ever since and will continue till I see it in reality. The Lord is true to His promise. With confidence in my heart, I know that a time is coming when the revival fires will sweep through the land of India and the nations of the world. With prayers and faith in our hearts, the world will see what God has promised. I believe it is a God-thing. It is not about techniques of ministry, great strategies, mesmerizing messages, charismatic leadership or intriguing rituals, magnificent buildings and structures that complicates Christianity. It is about the power of God to move according to His will. It is the supernatural work of the Holy Spirit.

I have only one goal in life, to make Jesus famous in my generation. The world must see it and God must be glorified. Amen.

Tampering With the Solar System

AS THE PASTOR OF THE CHURCH, I OFTEN RECEIVED phone calls from some frantic members as they faced overwhelming situations. While I found a great satisfaction when things turned out positively for them, I experienced a lot of stress seeing the intensity of their problems.

In the initial stages of my pastoral ministry, I prayed that I would have a stress free life. Then I realized that God had a different plan. God wanted me to be trained in various ways that were much different from the stress free life I would prefer. I decided to go ahead in the learning process that God had designed for me.

One evening, I received a frantic telephone call from a family who were members of the church. I knew they were expecting their second baby. As a church we had been praying for them. As Dr. Beaulah was having some complications in pregnancy, Jeyakumar wanted me to come over to their home that evening.

Knowing the situation they were experiencing, I was very apprehensive. As a pastor I realized I was being taken to places and had to face situations that were overwhelming and challenging. These situations challenged my faith, challenged my courage and eventually challenged everything about my life and ministry. To be honest, I felt drained emotionally and stressed beyond my comfort level. Invariably, every day was a day of crisis in someone's life.

To me, a crisis in a member's family became a personal crisis. I wondered if I should be involved to that extent in the lives of every member of my congregation? Should I stay aloof? Should I exhaust my life completely? Should I preserve my emotional strength and conserve my energy as many of the members had suggested? What should I do if they had a specific problem and came to me for help? Should I quote their advice to me in the past?

For answers I looked at the life of Jesus. He lived a quality life! He never preserved His life but gladly laid it down for others! I decided I would do the same if God would grant me such grace! I knew that God had called me for this very purpose.

Having reached this resolution to my apprehension, I was able to focus on the family who had requested my visit. The mother was probably into her fifth month of pregnancy. The doctors had advised her to abort the baby due to some complications. After examination, they detected abnormalities, possible problems in the heart, an abnormality in the development of limbs, and one kidney was undersized while the other one was only paper-thin. Surprisingly, the family stood up for what they believed and told the doctors that *whatever may happen to this child, we will accept this baby as a gift from God.* The doctors did not want to challenge this strange couple's stubborn faith and yet they were terrified to go through the ordeal of allowing the pregnancy to go to full term.

When I heard about all these things I did not have the courage to visit them. What advice could I offer? They had a greater faith than mine! I knew what I had to do. I would wait on the Lord. Surely God would provide the wisdom to deal with the situation. I disappeared into the privacy of a closed room and fell on my knees in prayer. Then I opened the Bible to find strength in the Word of God.

As I began to read the Bible, the Lord guided me to passage in Isaiah 38:5-8.

"Go and tell Hezekiah, 'this is what the Lord, the God of your father David, says: I have heard your prayer and seen your tears; I will add fifteen years to your life. And I will deliver you and this city from the hand of the king of Assyria. I will defend this city. This is the Lord's sign to you that the Lord will do what he has promised: I will make the shadow cast by the sun go back the ten steps it has gone down on the stairway of Ahaz."

And so, the sunlight went back the ten steps it had gone down!

It suddenly dawned on me that perhaps the Lord was telling me that he was going to perform a miracle for this family in this impossible situation. The king was not satisfied with an answered prayer in the form of an extended life even though he was sick unto death. He was asking for something that God himself could not do. Healing seemed easier compared to the sign given to encourage him to believe that he could have what God had promised. Could God tamper with His own solar system just because He wanted to give a king a sign? It seemed impossible. Maybe I ought to search for a better word. What word would suffice? I grasped the idea behind the whole thing.

With these words in my heart, Angie and I went over to see them. Now I needed the courage to tell them what I believed God had spoken to my heart. I found this to be a greater challenge. It is one thing to believe what the Bible says, but another thing altogether to speak it out in faith.

I struggled all the way as I drove the scooter through the incredible traffic in the city streets of Lucknow. We spent that whole evening with them listening to their hearts and crying to God along with them in prayer. Many people, including their own godly family, rallied around them providing them with great spiritual backing through out the whole time of trials. Then I shared with them from the Bible. I related the incident in the Bible and told them of the sign God had promised. God was willing to tamper with His solar system for them too! God had not changed. God's word had not changed. If we believe, God will prove His love and His power to us one more time. Late that night, we rode back home hoping and praying our lives had been useful and effective in the service of God.

As we saw them week after week in church, we came to hear some fascinating developments in their family. The mother had begun to see some remarkable improvements in the growth and development of the baby in the womb as she neared the time of delivery. The developments were phenomenal. The size of the limbs, the size of the kidneys and the strength that the baby was experiencing was beyond belief. We continued to pray for her every Sunday at the church. When the time was due, she delivered a normal and healthy baby boy. They celebrated the marvelous gift from God and named him, Matthew – Gift of Yahweh.

What an awesome and great God we worship! Indeed, He proved one more time that He is a God who is willing to tamper with His own solar system!

PART V

IMPACT BEYOND

THE CHURCH WALLS

Taking a Step of Faith

AT SOME POINT IN OUR SPIRITUAL JOURNEY, OUR lives and ministries merge into divine designs. They do not make sense when you view them separated from each other. To illustrate this, I want to share the transition that caused me to leave the pastorate and move to *Global Action*.

In January 2000, I had the privilege of meeting Lars Dunberg, the founding President of *Global Action*. He had arrived in Lucknow to conduct a three-day Pastors' Conference. Our church was asked to lead in worship during the conference so I took some young people and enjoyed the privilege.

A day after the conference, I was invited to join Lars and his son, Paul as they traveled to Kanpur, a twin city to Lucknow, to conduct a series of meetings for young people. As the entourage of cars was ready to leave, I found out that I would have Lars and Paul for company during the journey. Throughout the hours in the car, Lars shared his heart with me. I knew immediately that I was talking with a man who had a vision and passion for the Church of Jesus Christ. His spiritual journey simply captivated my heart. I felt small as I saw myself satisfied with a narrow vision for my life and ministry in relation to the needs in the kingdom of God. On our return journey, I shared my spiritual journey with Lars and Paul. Over the years I have come to realize that this particular journey was a divine appointment made by God.

Throughout my tenure in Lal Bagh Methodist Church, I had struggled in the pastoral ministry. I continually wondered when we would witness something beyond the local Church and when if ever we would see the bigger picture? Surely God must be doing something significant elsewhere too! It was then that things began to happen.

On a visit to my home church in Chennai in 1998, as a newly appointed pastor of the church, God spoke through Pastor James who said, "This appointment is not for a long time." At first I was upset. I had barely completed one-year of pastoral ministry in Lal Bagh.

In 2001, Meenu Chand, one of the young people in the youth fellowship, had a vision of Jesus with a torch in His hand standing taller than the steeple of our church. She told me that I was the torch in the hand of the Lord and that light was flowing out of that torch, reaching out to various parts of India. I was happy to interpret the vision by construing that God was going to make Lal Bagh Methodist Church like the church in Antioch, a place from which the name of Jesus would be spread out. I was going to be a catalyst. When students and outsiders came to the city the ministry at Lal Bagh benefited them. When they returned they shared the excitement of how God was using them in their own churches and in their own cities. It looked like the dream had a positive interpretation.

But in 2002, as I accepted the first invitation to teach in *Global Action*'s Global Module Studies program (GLOMOS), God showed me a huge door open in the sky and clearly told me that GLOMOS *is only a small step. There is something so big beyond it that you would not believe if it were told to you now.* I prayed over the dream. Over a period of time, God showed this same door to at least four different people in different times and places in confirmation of His word to me.

But, a battle raged within my heart. Again, I had questions. Am I contradicting myself? Did the Lord Himself bring me here to pastor these people? Will I be misunderstood if I change my mind? Can God so easily change His plan? Maybe this was part of His plan, which I had grossly misunderstood.

Lars started GLOMOS in Lucknow. In the year 2002, Lars provided me the first opportunity to teach in it. I was reluctant and spent time in prayer. Again I wondered if I wanted to be part of this because of the opportunity to travel by air, stay in hotels and make a name for myself? Or, is this really from God Himself? I prayed for quite a while.

In 2003, the Lord brought Kathleen back to Lucknow to encourage us. Angie and I spent time with her in her hotel. Through Kathleen the Lord told me to *put on your sandals* because He was going *to take me to many different places* and *dirty my feet.* Angie and I returned feeling perplexed.

In 2004, I had major heart surgery. I was out of action for three months. I missed the teaching opportunities but Lars called me and told me that he would like me to speak at a youth conference in Hyderabad in South India. I was thinking of my health, but he was looking at the health of the body of Jesus Christ. While I was barely out of hospital, I agreed to speak. Within four months, along with Lars and Galo Vasquez from Mexico, we had a phenomenal experience of leading, challenging and motivating over 1,300 young people to live for the Lord.

During one of the evenings, Lars asked me if I saw what he saw. "Is God showing you how you could be used in a great way to make a huge difference for people beyond the confines of a small church congregation in one city in India?" I chose to differ. I did not have any big plans for myself. As I have said before, I was not ambitious. Lars told me that I ought to think about and definitely pray about this possibility.

In 2005, Lars invited me to speak at a Pastors' Conference in Orissa and later in the year at another Youth Conference in the Himalayas. I suddenly began to see myself in different roles. I knew the Lord was leading me to something but I did not know what it was.

Both 2005 and 2006 were years of visions from the Lord. Very often I saw myself speaking and preaching in different countries. I began to write them down in my diary as I saw them. Russia, Eastern Europe, China, Korea, Malaysia, Singapore, England, Central America and the United States of America were some of the places I wrote down. It looked like God was teaching me geography in a night school. I began to let people in Lal Bagh know of the plans God was making for me. It was in line with the 43rd chapter of Isaiah, the same chapter brother John Joseph told me that God had asked him to give to me on the 13th of October 1983. A few days later, Annie Johnson told me God was showing her Isaiah 43:10 brightly lit on the pages of the Bible. I made it the theme and purpose of my life.

"You are my witnesses, declares the Lord, and my servant whom I have chosen, so that you may know and believe me and understand that I am he. Before me no god was formed, nor will there be one after me" (Isaiah 43:10).

I realized that I had been chosen to be a witness so that I may know Him, believe in Him, understand Him and share this experience to the ends of the earth. Nothing would give me a greater joy than to do just that. Everywhere I turned in the Bible, I found the Lord showing me that He would take me to the ends of the earth. How could this be? I was in a remote place in Lucknow. I concluded that either the Lord would do something supernatural so that Lucknow would be on the world map or He would take me to places I could not even imagine, to make Jesus famous.

Then the struggle intensified. I told Angie that what I was experiencing was similar to what I experienced when I was just about to leave the bank. I was apprehensive of making the move. The teaching opportunities were getting bigger. When I started in 2002, I only taught in one city. Now I was teaching in five cities. I was also speaking at Pastors' Conferences and Youth Conferences too. My cousin advised me that I ought to make the move. Lucknow was my Jerusalem, the other places were Judea and Samaria. Soon I would go the ends of the earth. I still could not make up my mind. Then I had a strange dream.

In my dream I saw myself talking to Lars. He was engaged in a serious conversation. He told me of how he saw me as one who was used by God in special ways that I was not even aware. Then he told me of the possibilities that *Global Action* would provide to impact the world with the Gospel of Jesus Christ. It could be through the youth and pastors' conferences where people were challenged to take the mission of God seriously. He talked about the training programs that could be held for pastors in specific countries to bring effectiveness in the ministry and revival of the churches. He told me that he was not in any way trying to disrupt what God was doing in my life as a pastor or in the church. All he wanted was to offer the opportunity to facilitate the plan of God for my life, since he saw it in line with what *Global Action* wanted to do. He told me he was not pushing me to make a specific decision. If it were from God, then he would be happy to take a "yes." But, if not, he would accept "no." If I needed more time he was willing to wait. I jumped out of bed only to realize it was a dream.

Then I had another dream. This time I saw Bishop Thomas calling me over in a large auditorium. He put a stole around my neck and offered a higher position within the Church. I saw myself nodding my head and saying "no" to the opportunity.

This was followed by another dream in which Lars told me, "Sundar, if this is what you feel in your heart, you must talk to your Bishop and see what he thinks about it." I was still not sure.

One day I received a phone call from Lars. He said he was passing by India and would love to stop over in Lucknow for a day and meet with us. I told him that I would like to bring Angie along.

When we met with him, Lars began to share his concerns and the vision God had put in his heart. He also discussed further the possibility of me joining *Global Action* if that was the will of God for the organization and me. When we had finished, I told Lars that I had heard the entire conversation verbatim in a dream that the Lord had shown to me. In my heart I knew that this was the plan of God for my life and this was the man God would have to mentor me into the next phase of my ministry. Still I chose to remain silent about a decision and pray about it.

Then I had another dream. I saw myself walking along the edge of a mountain overlooking the sea. Great waves came and lashed at the rocks at the base of the mountain. Then I saw myself climbing higher along a dangerous trail. The sea below looked deep blue and, as I climbed higher, I was a bit dizzy. Suddenly the slope in the mountain had steps carved out of the rock just ahead of me. I was unwilling to climb any further as I sensed the dangers that lay ahead. It was too risky now. Then I heard a voice from behind, "Take a step of faith." With much hesitation I took a feeble step. As I continued the flight of steps carved out of the rock, I suddenly discovered that the steps had no connection with the mountain any more. They seemed to be suspended in air. Again I heard the voice, "Take a step of faith." As I took the step of faith, out of nowhere another one appeared before me. I realized that I was walking by faith. Finally I had no step to put my foot on. Again the voice guided me. I took another one only to find myself plunge with great speed down toward the sea. The wind whistled past as I went down. An invisible hand seemed to carry me just as I hit the surface of the sea below. It was an exhilarating experience. I enjoyed what was going on. I said to myself, "What a great experience. Why have I not taken the step earlier?"

Later that year in 2006, a team arrived from New York. One of the team members met me and said, "Young man, I see the anointing of the Lord upon you. Millions are waiting to be ministered by you. You will soon travel the world to preach Christ to them." I had already decided to make the decision but wondered how I could take on bigger responsibilities. Again, I was plagued with questions. Was I capable? How would it affect me? I wished someone would help and share the responsibilities.

With this mindset I went to attend a one day Pastors' Seminar in Lucknow. I was seated in the front row of the auditorium as the day's program got underway. Lennarth Hambre, one of *Global Action*'s board members and the former president of the Evangelical Free Church of Sweden, was there to speak. Suddenly he said, "I have a word from the Lord for someone." As he began to speak I started to remove my shoes. Angie asked me what I was doing. I told her I felt that the Lord was going to speak to me. Then Lennarth looked directly at me and said, "You are like Moses. Take a step of faith. Do not hesitate. You are wondering how you would do the work God has called you to do. God will provide an Aaron to help you."

Now the matter was sealed without a doubt. Angie and I went to see the Bishop. Being a kindhearted man he listened to our story with much understanding and then told us, "I knew a day like this would come. I have heard you preach several times. I knew the local church would not hold you too long. You have my blessings. Take a break from the pastoral ministry and be a blessing to the world." Later the Bishop said the same thing to the congregation at Lal Bagh as well.

I joined *Global Action* in May 2007 through a series of events that were ordained by God and in obedience to the call of God on my life. What a joy it has been since then to experience Jesus in unique ways.

GLOMOS - The Answer to
An Exploding Church

SOMETIME BETWEEN 2002 AND 2003, I MET A GLOMOS student in Delhi who had an interesting story.

At the beginning of a module I like to ask the students where they come from. Normally, each student will indicate which part of Delhi he or she resides. But, one student responded, "I am from London." When I inquired as to why he came from London, the student told his story to the class.

> *"Sir, it so happened that my family migrated to London some months ago. It was a move planned earlier. One day my wife found me somewhat crest-fallen. She asked, 'Are you not happy?' 'Do you miss home?' I answered her, 'No! It's just that I miss the GLOMOS classes. How I wish I could go back to India and attend the remaining modules and graduate.' My wife said, 'If it is so important to you, I think you must!' I was astonished at her encouragement considering the financial implications. So here I am. This is my fourth visit to India. I am going to miss GLOMOS since I will now be graduating."*

I was challenged! I prayed, "If this is the desire for a student to learn, Lord, help me to give my best as a teacher."

I was invited to speak at a Missions Seminar held in Gurgoan, near Delhi, in October 2007. On the first day, I met a young man, Mr. Rocky (M.K. Raj). He said, "Sir, I knew you were coming and I was eagerly waiting to see you."

I asked, "What are you doing here?"

"Sir", he replied, "I am a missionary with the Delhi Bible Fellowship."

I asked, "How come?"

"It was because I attended the GLOMOS in Delhi and also because you were my teacher."

Incidentally, Raj is a karate champion and an international referee. He was challenged to be a risk-taker for God while attending GLOMOS and is now in full-time ministry working among children. He visits various places and offers to teach martial arts free of charge. After the session, he gathers the children to tell them stories of Jesus Christ and teaches them new songs. His ministry was launched as he was leading these children to salvation through Jesus Christ.

In Kolkata in 2005, I met another student, Dipaankar. He seemed to answer all the questions that were raised by me during the GLOMOS class. I initially thought he was overpowering everyone with his display of Bible knowledge. Then it dawned on me that I was sadly mistaken.

When I had asked of his amazing knowledge of the Bible and how long he had been a believer, he answered, "I am a baby!"

Surprised, I asked, "What do you mean?" This is his story.

"Sir, when I was 15 I got into bad company. In one of our troubled days someone was killed. I was implicated. They handed out a life-sentence to me. While I was in prison, a man came and shared that there is forgiveness for every sin and that it is available only through Jesus Christ. I was interested in the message and began to believe in Christ. Later on when I met the man, I told him how Jesus had changed my life and how I enjoyed peace with God. I then asked the man if Jesus could do another miracle for me? Can he get me out of prison?

"The man encouraged me to believe since with God nothing is impossible. So we prayed together. After the next few months, one day I was surprisingly summoned to the office. They told me that they were able to see such a remarkable change in my behavior and believed that I did not deserve to be in prison. They told me they would move my file to the higher authorities for favorably considering my situation. Although nothing was promised, I was soon released on a presidential pardon!

"I desired to study the Bible and it was then that I came to know about the GLOMOS program. Sir, now I am a daily wage laborer and my wife is a dance teacher. Our family has disowned us but with the little we have, we are happy. I regularly share the gospel with other people."

Three years later I met Dipaankar again. He invited me to come and preach in the church he had planted. They now have put up a structure and he no longer lives on the streets of Kolkata. GLOMOS has enabled him to find his vocation, change his location and more importantly, discover the purpose of his life.

When I met Bidesh Singh, he had been led to the Lord only a year before but, he has a great passion to share his faith with others. They told me that he was planning something big. During the Kolkata GLOMOS he narrated his story.

Bidesh was an ardent Hindu who, when he came to believe in Christ, wanted first of all to share his faith with his temple priest. He went to the village and told the priest that salvation cannot be found in Hinduism. The priest casually replied that he knew that. Bidesh then asked, "Why are you working in this temple?"

"Well, this is just my job and I have to earn a living!" the priest replied.

Bidesh then shared his faith in Jesus Christ with him. Later on, Bidesh pleaded with the village leaders so that he could be given an opportunity to share his faith with the people of his village. With their consent, he individually knocked on the doors of the homes of villagers and gathered 1,500 people in one place.

Bidesh told me that the GLOMOS training had given him the boldness and the truth to share his convictions with the people. What a passion! His story shows how God often uses ordinary people to accomplish enormous tasks.

In the GLOMOS program up in the foothills of the Himalayas in Kalimpong, I met another student whose testimony challenged me. Nirvan traveled 50 miles on foot to get to the center where GLOMOS was being held. During the break-time, I wanted to verify the facts. He told me this amazing story!

Until three years ago, Nirvan was a Hindu. But now he had given his life to Christ. During these past three years, Nirvan had shared his testimony and led many people to Christ. He became their pastor. I asked him how he could possibly make that distance to reach the center on foot. He replied, "This is not a problem. Since I have established five churches in three years, I have my services on the weekdays. Since every church is situated 30 miles apart, I need to cover that distance every day.

This means climbing the mountains, crossing the rivers, walking and running too. I have the services from Monday through Friday. We don't meet on Saturday and Sunday!"

I marveled at his commitment. How could a person establish five churches in three years and do that without any training? Sometimes it is the student himself who challenges the teachers! God has indeed chosen the weak and the foolish things to confound the strong and the wise!

I met another student who had a great story. He came to GLOMOS because someone recommended it to him. At that time he only wanted to gain some knowledge of the Bible. While attending the courses in the GLOMOS program, he realized that he must do it with all his heart. So when he went back home he decided to take care of people's financial needs and in his own small way do something for God. What started as a small, sacrificial effort turned out to become a small group. He spent his own money and took his small group members to doctors for treatment. Soon people saw his concern and were added to the group. With the GLOMOS training he began to teach them and encouraged them to pray fervently.

Now the group has grown to become a full-fledged church. He uses all the resources he received at the GLOMOS training. His church is now growing stronger and stronger. Eventually, he became the pastor of the congregation. He shared how it was amazing to see the hand of the Lord upon the people of his congregation. What had started as a desire to gain knowledge developed into a church with people excited to live for Christ.

Orissa has been in the headlines of Indian newspapers and also in the global headlines for the kind of persecution that has been unleashed in the past years. During GLOMOS graduation ceremony, I saw one of the students sporting long hair. I casually remarked that he looked like Jesus in the movie, *Jesus of Nazareth*. He replied that it was for that very purpose he had changed his hairstyle. He is part of a group of believers who take the Gospel of Jesus Christ to the villages. He plays the role of Jesus in street plays. I had met him a few times and I knew that only a couple of years ago he got married. I asked him if it was risky to attempt such a thing when the persecution had not yet died down. He replied, "Sir, this is the right time to do it. It is now that the people who oppose the Gospel need to hear it." With a broad smile I saw his wife nodding her head in support of her husband's stand for Christ. This newly married couple is the kind of risk-takers for God that *Global Action* desires to see!

Another student narrated this experience. He was the first one in his family and his entire community to come to believe in Christ. For this they hated him and eventually disowned him. They cursed him for turning his back on their gods and said that something dreadful would happen to him. Soon he fell sick and was completely bedridden for a period of two years. But he never gave up. Rather he trusted God!

He told his family that Jesus would heal him and that he would walk again without having to undergo any kind of surgery. Sure enough, he got up one fine day and began to testify to the living reality of Jesus Christ. In spite of having to face much rejection and ridicule, he continued to pray for the salvation of his family members. Soon four of his brothers and their families trusted in Jesus Christ for their salvation. With joy he graduated from GLOMOS this year. He is now trained to teach the gospel more effectively. He even composed several poems and has been given an opportunity to have them printed in a national magazine periodical!

I met this GLOMOS alumnus in the *Global Action* Lucknow office one day. It was obvious from the look on his face that he was excited for Jesus Christ. He said, "Sir, I have been waiting to tell you of the marvelous manner in which I am experiencing the hand of God in our ministry. I work on the outskirts of the city of Lucknow. I have been praying for a breakthrough in our ministry. I have toiled hard all these years facing opposition, but now I know my prayers are being heard. I went to visit a man so that I could pray for him. His family has opposed me for several years. Soon I realized that if God would perform a miracle I could win this family and also have the breakthrough that I am looking for.

As I prayed for this man, I realized that he was not only bedridden but demon-possessed as well. So I prayed with the family and told them to trust in Jesus Christ. After several hours of intercession, the demons fled from him. I told this bed-ridden man that Jesus would heal him and make him walk again.

At first, the family could not believe what I had said. I prayed for a breakthrough in the family. After five and a half hours of praying, the Lord revealed His power and the man began to sit upright and then began to walk. The family, who would not believe, now could not turn away from Christ. The Lord brought salvation to the entire household! Now the church is growing and God has done many more miracles and is adding new believers to the church."

Let's Stop and Pray!

IN 2008 I WAS GIVEN THE OPPORTUNITY TO VISIT HONduras, teaching in the GLOMOS program with the goal to equip pastors and leaders with skills and knowledge to increment effectiveness in their ministry. The topic I was given to teach was *The Uniqueness of Jesus Christ*.

At the outset I knew I was not the expert on the subject. I also knew that the scope of the topic was wide. I trembled on the inside with fear. I spent more time praying than preparing to teach the subject. I told the Lord that the best thing that could happen at the end of it all was to experience the supernatural Jesus Christ who we wanted to learn from. What we learn in the classroom must be something that we experience in our daily lives. It was not just about imparting information. Therefore, the teaching should lead to transformation.

I decided that I needed to share openly with the students the kind of experiences that people, including myself, have had that make the learning process challenging and stimulating. I have always communicated the gospel that way so it was not something new I was attempting. I introduced myself and dove into the subject.

The first day went well. This was my first experience teaching in another country. Slowly my confidence grew and I became more comfortable. The second day was about the life and ministry of Jesus Christ. By this time I had shared with them everything I possibly knew, along with the experiences of Jesus Christ in peoples' lives. I must confess that I had begun to actually enjoy the time of teaching.

When the afternoon session came, the director of the program in Honduras, Liliana Bendana, told me that she felt the need for a time of prayer with the students. I was reluctant since I was not prepared for it. Her good sense prevailed and we decided to take some time out of our teaching for prayer.

I asked them to sing a couple of songs while I cried my heart out to the Lord in prayer. I pleaded that God would forgive me of whatever sin I had committed and then continued to plead that I would not be the hindrance to the blessing He would have for the students that day. Then we went into prayer. Those with special prayer requests lined up in front as I prayed for them individually. After having prayed for at least four of them, I moved to pray for the fifth person.

She requested that she be filled with the Holy Spirit so that she could continue her ministry in a more powerful manner. I said, "Lord, this woman is asking for the best gift you could give. You promised that the Heavenly Father himself would give it to anyone who asks of Him." Then I placed my hand on her head and said, "In the name of Jesus, the name above all names in heaven and on earth and under the earth and the authority that God has granted to me as His servant, receive the power of the Holy Spirit." Suddenly she was thrown four feet and fell backwards.

At that moment I felt a supernatural power take control of me. I quickly moved into the group and raised my hands in prayer for each and every person in the class. I blessed them with the mighty anointing of the Holy Spirit so that they could advance the kingdom of God. I prayed for the protection of their marriages and families as well. Then I continued to pray for the others who were still waiting. We finished the time allotted for prayer and then took a brief tea break.

When we returned to commence the final session for the day, Liliana wanted to use the time for people to share their testimonies of what they experienced during the time of prayer. It sounded good and I was hoping as usual to hear something so that I too could be encouraged. One lady came and said, "When Pastor Moses prayed for my back, he said, 'In the name of Jesus, receive your healing.' I felt a strange warmth in my back. Then I heard a cracking sound. It was the same sound that I had heard when I fell from a flight of stairs years before when I was in the seventh month of my pregnancy. Praise the Lord, the fall did not affect the child, but I have been in pain for the past seven years. Today when I heard the sound, I realized God put my back in place again. I have no pain." She jumped for joy as we celebrated her miracle.

The next lady said, "I was suffering for the past two years with no blood flow in my right leg. I could feel nothing below my knee. When I shared it with Rev. Moses, he knelt down and placed his hand on my leg and said, 'In the name of Jesus, I command the blood to flow.' Praise the Lord. At that very instant I felt the sudden gushing of blood right down to my ankles and toes. When the class took the tea break, I went to the rest room to check my condition. It is true. I could feel the floor." She also jumped for joy as she could not contain herself any longer.

The next man was a pastor and he began telling his story. "I had hurt my back and have been in immense pain for the past two years. Without help and assistance from my wife I cannot retire to bed or rise up in the morning on my own. Every day I told myself I would be healed by the Lord miraculously. Yesterday when I heard the testimonies, I knew my time had come. Now I am without pain and intend to serve the Lord even more."

As the other testimonies were shared, I felt that there was someone in the class who had experienced something deeply but did not share it with the others. When there was no response, I felt I must point out that person myself. I said to one of them, "You are the person!" She came up to the front with tears. "I can't hide anything anymore," she cried. "I have been deeply grieved over the developments in our church. My family has been going through much heartache. We are not able to cope with the misunderstandings we are experiencing. It has divided two families in the church and at this moment our daughters are caught up in the same things. I am sorry for the pain it has caused the body of Christ." I told her that God would forgive her and reconcile the families. I asked her to mention the name of the person so that we could pray for him. Then she told us it was her pastor! He was also attending this same class, going through the training program along with her. He came up and asked for forgiveness and the two of them hugged each other and reconciled in front of all the other students. I thought the session had concluded. But God was not finished yet.

At this moment Liliana told us that she needed to be reconciled with someone. I admired the humility that she displayed. The next person came up and said that he too wanted to forgive some people who had plotted to kidnap his son. One by one they came forward to confess their sins and seek forgiveness and reconciliation. There was so much emotion. People were crying and hugging each other. It was nothing but a God-ordained moment. We concluded for the day.

I returned to my room to recollect the wonderful things that God had done for these special people at GLOMOS in Honduras. The next day we talked about the trial and crucifixion of Jesus Christ. The Spirit of God moved in our midst. Students wept as the Lord brought such conviction in their lives. It was a thoroughly enjoyable experience. God indeed had heard my prayer, "Lord enable us to be revived."

When Two or Three Are Gathered In His Name

IN 2008 I HAD THE PRIVILEGE TO GO TO EL SALVADOR for the first time. I was scheduled to teach in the GLOMOS program on the same subject I had taught in Honduras, *The Uniqueness of Jesus Christ.*

When I landed in Honduras the week before, I felt as if no one knew me in Latin America so I could enjoy anonymity. As the pastor of a church in Lucknow I had become well known in India and my reputation always had an indirect pressure on the way I lived my life. Honduras was a great relief in that sense. However, when I landed in El Salvador things seemed to change.

The director of the program in El Salvador, Mercedes Dalton, is the sister of Liliana in Honduras. She had been updated on the miraculous things the Lord had done just a couple of days prior to my coming to El Salvador. At the outset she told me that she too would like to have a session of prayer with the students in her program.

The first day went well as we looked at the background of Jesus. Briefly we studied the political, social, economical and religious background in order to understand Jesus and His teaching in the right context. Then we studied the Old Testament as a preparation to receive Jesus Christ. We looked at His unique birth, His childhood and then covered the period of His ministry. As this was a topic I cherished deeply, I communicated it passionately. We talked about His power over demons, diseases and disasters. We talked of His unique doctrines. We studied how He accepted the devotion of a woman and how He cleared the doubts of John the Baptist in a unique manner. Then we took a break for lunch.

In the afternoon session we talked about the unjust civil and religious trials that Jesus had to undergo before He was brutally crucified on a Roman cross. As we completed that discussion, I was asked to spend the next session in prayer with them. My heart was racing within me. Were the things that happened in Honduras a rare incident? Was it just a flash in the pan? I cried to God for His mercy. "Remember us, Lord, and show us who you are. Should you be relegated to the pages of the Scripture? If so, the Bible is just a history book. If we can experience you today, then we can consider it to be a theological one. What good is it to be trapped into the confines of an era gone by, because of our theological mindset? Theology must set our mind free to enjoy and experience God. Holy Spirit, come and have your way in our midst. Lead us to deeper truths that can transform our lives."

As usual I told them to sing a couple of songs to prepare our hearts for what God would have for us during this time. Then I told them what the Bible declares in Matthew 18:20. *"For where two or three come together in my name, there am I with them."* I also reminded them that Jesus promised to be with us and that He will come and when He comes He will do miraculous things.

As I began to get into the deeper things of the Spirit, I felt like I was standing next to a pillar of fire. It emanated blazing heat. I felt my head; my right arm and ears were about to be singed with that heat. I knew the Lord was with us in person so I declared to the students, "As the servant of the Living God I declare to you that the Lord is in our midst right now. If you believe, you will receive. If you need to be prayed over, come and receive the blessing of God."

When I opened my eyes I was surprised to see all 85 students file into a single line. Then I began to pray, saying, "Lord, these hands have committed sins against you. I have been an enemy of God most of my life. What good can come out of this exercise? As I place my hands on these dear people of God, may it be symbolic of the sinless and sacred hands of Jesus Christ. It is from you that anything good can really happen."

Then I felt a rare sensation. Every time I placed my hands on someone I felt another gentle but powerful hand placed over mine. People buckled under the touch. Many broke down in tears. Others trembled even as they approached me. I knew it could not be me. I knew something supernatural was taking place. Arterial blockages in someone's heart were cleared instantaneously. The man, who could not afford his medical treatment, was bubbling with joy as he took in his first breath of air in a long time. God gave many a pastor a fresh unction to do ministry.

When we had finished more than two hours had gone by. It was a physically draining time but spiritually uplifting too. As I sat down exhausted, one of the students told me what she had witnessed.

"When you had begun the prayer and told us that Jesus would come in order to keep the promise He had made, I felt something happen. So I opened my eyes to see what was going on. I saw Jesus standing at the entrance of the room. When you told us that Jesus was standing next to us, I saw Jesus walking through the middle of the room to stand next to you." It was at that time I had experienced such intense heat and encouraged the students to come and receive the blessing that Jesus had for them. Then she continued telling me that as I pleaded with the Lord to place His hands over them—since my human and sinful hands could not help them—she saw Jesus place His hand over every person on whom I laid hands and prayed for. I felt I was the one who was blessed the most during that day.

This experience has changed the way I look at things. Should we take the verses in the Bible and look at them critically or should we choose to believe His word?

Lord, forgive us the formality of worship. Open our eyes that we may see you. Unplug our ears that we may hear you and gain access to your will and may we worship you in Spirit and in Truth.

He Can Do Withouth Preaching

DURING MY FIRST VISIT TO HONDURAS IN 2008, THE Lord performed so many supernatural miracles. I returned to India with great satisfaction in my heart that God had revealed Himself in new ways and that I had fresh experiences with Him that would help keep us on the right path throughout our spiritual journey.

I have always maintained that a Christian must have new testimonies in his or her life. I shared these stories to challenge people to believe the Bible and experience God in special ways. My travel took me to new places: Nepal, Sri Lanka and Canada. Everywhere I delighted myself in talking about the Uniqueness of Jesus Christ. Everything else needed to take a back seat. Throughout the year God gave me opportunities to do just that.

A year later I returned to Honduras to conduct the same teaching to a new class of students. When I arrived at the airport my interpreter, Edy and his wife Amy, came to welcome me back to Honduras. They told me that I needed to speak the next day and also wanted me to meet with their pastor. It was a Thursday prayer meeting in the church. They wanted me to share something on prayer. I was reluctant, since I had already been traveling for three weeks by that time. I was saving some energy for my teaching responsibilities.

When I arrived at the church, I was surprised to see so many people. I wondered what made them come to attend a weekly prayer service at the church. Then the pastor told me that the people had come to see me. Why me? It was because of what had happened during my previous visit. I tried to remember. I recalled that as I was traveling to the airport to begin the long journey back home, I was asked to meet the pastor of this church and pray for him. I also remembered that there was a group of young people practicing for the Sunday worship service. The pastor requested that I pray for them. I prayed, "Lord, please bless these young people. As they use their God-given abilities to lead the people in worship, may your anointing fall on them and may you use them in supernatural ways. Let the skills be divinely orchestrated and their voices be harmonized too. Let the people know that you are the reason for the worship. Fill every heart with a spirit of worship." That was the quick prayer I made as I hurried to the airport.

Then the pastor shared what had happened after I left. The following Sunday as the congregation came together, the service got underway. The worship team began to lead along with the musicians. Suddenly many in the congregation began weeping. Some fell on their knees in prayer. Others walked up to the altar and lay prostrate, weeping. The pastor urged the worship team to continue beyond the specified time. He counseled and led people to repentance and faith in Jesus Christ. Then he apologized to the congregation that he could not find time in the service to preach the word of God. The service then concluded.

The following Sunday the same thing happened all over again. As the worship team led the service, people began to weep and the pastor helped them to find forgiveness and salvation through Jesus Christ. For the second week running he apologized for not preaching. This phenomenon occurred over the next two or three weeks. The pastor led so many of his congregation to the Lord. He told me that people now wanted to know the man from India who had prayed in the church before he returned home. As they shared this in front of the congregation, I broke down in tears. I was amazed to learn how the Lord had worked miraculously in that church. I realized He can do without our preaching!

Full Circle

IN 2010, I HAD THE OPPORTUNITY TO VISIT EL SALVAdor for the third time. By now the venue was moved to Santa Ana, a city situated about an hour from San Salvador. I was excited to have the opportunity to teach. There were about one hundred students present in the church where the class was held. I made friends with the pastor, Mauro Antonio Ayala, and recalled that he, along with his wife, had been students in the program the previous year.

Since I had been meeting with people in this country before, the evenings became rather busy. Late into the night people came to be prayed for. It was tiring, especially after a whole day of teaching, but it was satisfying to speak about Jesus even if it meant late into the night.

On the second night, the pastor asked me to spend some time with his children, so he came over to pick me up and asked me if I would like to spend our time with his kids or to see the city at night. I preferred to spend time with his family. They were a lovely family and I enjoyed the evening with them. As we entered the parking lot, I shared with him about how God used me to be a link in a chain of events. And this is that story.

In 2009, I had concluded teaching in Honduras. On the final day one of the students came over to me and tucked a twenty-dollar bill in my hand. I told him I did not need it and that since he himself was a pastor, he should keep it. He insisted I take it. Then he told me that this is a sign of what the Lord is going to do from now on. He continued telling me that the Lord says, "People whom you do not know will place money in your hands. Through these hands of yours the Lord will bless people in need." I took a picture of the twenty-dollar bill and moved on to El Salvador to teach. As the three days came to an end, I stayed back to talk to people and pray with them. As we finished the classes there was great excitement among the students. I was glad I could come over to Central America to invest in the lives of these pastors, church leaders and Christian workers. All of them wished me well as they left the GLOMOS course.

One of them came to me and said, "Pastor Moses, you talked about someone in the city of Kolkata who lives on the pavement. I would like to give something right away. This is all I have at the moment." He quickly removed the gold ring from his finger and tucked it into an envelope and handed it over to me. "Please sell it and hand over the money to him."

I could not believe the event. Just a couple of days earlier I had this student in GLOMOS in Honduras prophesy over my life specifically in this regard. Now it was already happening in El Salvador. I told the person who gave me the ring to kindly write down his name and his email address so that I could let him know what I did with the ring he gave me. He said that he could trust me with that ring. On returning to India, I was happy to get it converted into cash. I went to Kolkata with the money and traced the GLOMOS student I had described in Honduras and wrote the testimony on a piece of paper and explained how it all happened. I was happy to be a link in the chain of events. The pastor in Kolkata was so happy to receive the financial help and thanked God for the gift. I wished I could convey his thanks.

When I went out with this pastor's family that night I shared the miraculous sequence of events that had taken place during my earlier visit to Central America. As I shared, there were tears of joy in the pastor's eyes. I wanted to know what had moved his heart with such emotion. He called his wife to come and then they told me it was he who had dropped the ring into my hand the previous year! My prayer had been answered. I had always intended to tell the person who had given the ring to me what I had done with it. At this very moment I was explaining it to him in person! What a highlight of my life! It is a great privilege to be one of the links in the supernatural things that God does in the lives of His people. What a great feeling!